Exploring Ephesians
an Expository Commentary

EXPLORING EPHESIANS
An Expository Commentary

Written by
Talbert W. Swan, II, Th.M.

Trumpet in Zion Publishing
Indian Orchard, MA

EXPLORING EPHESIANS

An Expository Commentary

by

Talbert W. Swan, II, Th.M.

Copyright 2003 by Trumpet in Zion Publishing

All rights reserved

Printed in the United States of America.

No part of this book may be reproduced, stored in a retrieval system, or transmitted by any means, electronic, mechanical, photocopying, recording or otherwise, without written permission from the author.

All Scripture References are the New King James Version (NKJV)

For information:

Trumpet in Zion Publishing
P.O. Box 51163
Indian Orchard, MA 01151

Web site: www.tzpublishing.com

Library of Congress Control Number: 2002096404

ISBN 0-9716355-5-2

DEDICATION

To Whitney, Shannon, Eryca, and Drystal. You are God's gifts to my life. Each of you are precious in the sight of God. You are blessed, and highly favored. Don't ever settle for less than what a Queen deserves.

- Love Dad

CONTENTS

Introduction 1

Chapter 1: Redemption and Adoption 14

Chapter 2: Grace Through Faith 29

Chapter 3: Glory and Power 41

Chapter 4: Spiritual Gifts 52

Chapter 5: How to Walk 71

Chapter 6: The Whole Armor of God 95

Fast Facts on the Book of Ephesians 116

Figures 121

Exploring Ephesians: An Expository Commentary

INTRODUCTION

Of all the books in the Bible, Ephesians best encompasses all of Christian thought and life. It not only tells us of our blessings and position in Christ, but also guides us in our day to day living. Some of Paul's letters arose from specific circumstances; e.g., Colossians is written to correct doctrinal error. Ephesians seems to be a letter springing from Paul's desire that the believers should be fully grounded in the profound doctrines of the gospel and faithfully geared to live victorious lives for Christ. It is a guidebook for emotional, mental, relational and spiritual wellbeing.

Chapters 1 – 3 describe the spiritual blessings of adoption, redemption, acceptance, wisdom, inheritance, forgiveness, life, grace, citizenship, and the seal of the Holy Spirit. Chapters 4 – 6 teaches the believer to walk in the spirit through the spiritual wealth given to us by God.

AUTHORSHIP

Evidence support the Pauline authorship of Ephesians. In the sixteenth century Erasmus questioned whether Paul wrote this epistle because he thought he detected differences in style between it and the other epistles. It was not, however, until the nineteenth century that Paul's authorship was seriously questioned. The objections are rather weak and have been answered adequately by competent scholars. The internal evidence strongly favors Pauline authorship. The epistle itself claims to have

Introduction

been written by Paul, and it is his theology throughout, although it does contain some new concepts related to the church. The structure of the epistle is definitely Pauline. A stronger case can be presented for Pauline authorship from the language standpoint than can be made against it. The external evidence for Pauline authorship is also substantial.

The construction of the Epistle follows Paul's pattern. The language is also Paul's. Some scholars have pointed out that there are 43 words found only in Ephesians and not in any of Paul's other Epistles. There are also 42 words in Ephesians that are not found anywhere else in the New Testament. The answer is that most of his Epistles have words that are unique to them. Careful observation will reveal that the same scholars who try to discredit Pauline authorship of Ephesians by comparing its word usage with other Pauline Epistles generally do not accept the other Pauline Epistles as authentic either. Since the epistle clearly names its author, it is unnecessary to theorize that Ephesians was written by anyone other than Paul.

WRITTEN TO WHOM

Many scholars think that Paul wrote the letter as a circular letter to all of the churches of Asia, but it came to be generally known as the letter to the Ephesians early on because Ephesus was the major city of Asia. Therefore, they think, early scribes inserted "in Ephesus" into the text. (Many older manuscripts do not contain these words.) A circular letter means it was originally written to a group of churches and circulated among them. There are some very excellent reasons to support this thinking.

One reason is that this epistle does not have any personal greetings in it. Paul had spent three years in Ephesus and had developed a long-term relationship with this church. In his epistles he almost always greets friends and colleagues. We would have expected him in an epistle written to a specific church where he knew so many people to have greeted some of the people personally. Since the phrase "at Ephesus" was added in the second century, it is very likely that the epistle was written to a group of churches and Ephesus was the chief church in the region. It is almost certain that during Paul's stay in Ephesus the territory around the city was evangelized and new churches were started.

DATE AND PLACE OF WRITING

The date of the writing is early in Paul's first Roman imprisonment. It is thought that Paul wrote a group of epistles called the "Prison Epistles" at the time of his imprisonment in Rome: Ephesians, Philippians (1:7), Colossians (4:10) and Philemon. Ephesians is placed in this time period because of its similarities to Colossians and Philemon and the probability that Tychicus delivered both letters (Ephesians. 6:21-22; Col. 4:7-9). Ephesians gives no hint of Paul's release from prison as do Philippians (1:19-26) and Philemon. It may well have been written in the early part of his stay, or around A.D. 60 or 61.

PURPOSE OF WRITING

Paul's purpose in writing Ephesians is to teach what it means to be "in Christ," what the church's role and responsibility is as the body of Christ, and how all

Introduction

things find their unity in Christ. Christ is the head of the church, and the church is his body. Since the church is his body, Christ is not complete without the church. The church, is composed of God's people, who have been redeemed by Jesus death on the cross. Paul motivates the believer to draw upon spiritual sources in daily living and to "walk worthy of the calling with which you were called" (4:1).

Paul does not write this letter to the Ephesians to rebuke them for any irregularity of conduct, like he does the Corinthians, nor for any perversion of the gospel, as he does the Galatians. His letter was one of joyous praise for God's eternal purpose. As such, it would serve as an antidote to the pagan mystery religions which were all around them, and to the arguments of the Judaizers who would be using all their powers of persuasion to impress these former pagans, who had prided themselves as guardians of the great Temple of Diana, with the pomp and ceremony of Judaism, along with its Jerusalem Temple. But why, someone might ask, did God permit Judaism and the pagan mystery religions to exist so long before He revealed the gospel? Was the gospel simply an afterthought of God? Absolutely not! God was working out His eternal plan for the redemption of mankind in Christ Jesus. In fact, the leading thought of this letter is: "The church of Jesus Christ, in which Jew and Gentile are made one, is a creation of the Father, through the Son, in the Holy Spirit, decreed from eternity, and destined for eternity."

In chapters 1-3, Paul shows that the church was foreordained by God, that it has been redeemed, and that Jew and Gentile have been made one in Christ. It is here that he lists the believer's heavenly possessions: adoption, redemption, inheritance, life, grace, power, citizenship, and the seal of the Holy Spirit. In chapters 4-6, Paul embarks upon the practical application of the truth stated in the first three chapters. He writes of unity, love, newness of life, walking in the strength of the Lord, and the need to put on the armor of God. These chapters also give directives that speak to the believers responsibility to engage in appropriate conduct.

Consequently, there is a clear-cut division in this letter between the *exposition* found in these first three chapters and the *exhortation* found in chapters 4-6. In chapters 1-3, the truth is *stated*; in chapters 4-6, the truth is *applied*. The theology of chapters 1--3 focuses upon the need for the Ephesians to increase in their awareness of God's love so that they will imitate it to God's glory. The applications of chapters 4--6 are specific expressions of love for one another in view of God's love. Paul is encouraging the church to maintain their position of unity.

A BRIEF OVERVIEW

The epistle itself is divided into two sections, of three chapters each. The first section is doctrinal and the second is practical. In the first, Paul deals with Christian truth, belief, and in the second he deals with the Christian life, behavior. In chapters 1-3, Paul presents the blessing the believers have in Christ. In the last chapters,4-6, Paul deals with the believer's life in the world. Verse 1 of Chapter 4 has the phrase "to walk worthy." The word translated "worthy" is axiwv. The English word "axis" comes from this word. The dictionary defines axis as "any lengthwise central

Introduction

line around which parts of a body are symmetrically arranged."

The idea is the Christians belief and behavior are to be balanced. It is the concept of an equal sign with the equation on each side balanced. Paul is saying live your life equal to the blessings God has given you. The believer is seated on the throne with Jesus Christ in the heavenlies; therefore, he can walk in purity and love in the world, but separate from the world. Therefore, Paul concludes, there is harmony and unity within the family between the husband and wife and between parents and children.

THE CITY OF EPHESUS

If the letter was intended for Ephesus, then it is helpful to know something of Paul's relationship with this great metropolis. Ephesus was a leading center in the Roman Empire. By the middle of the second millennium B.C., settlers of Asiatic origin inhabited the site. During the eleventh century B.C., Athenians arrived and gradually assimilated the older population. After varying periods of independence and absorption into neighboring empires, Ephesus came into the Roman Empire in 133 B.C. as part of the province of Asia. It enjoyed great prosperity under Rome during the first and second centuries A.D., when the city must have had a population of about a half million. It was here that the Roman governor resided and where Paul conducted the longest of his city ministries (two years and nine months (Acts 19:8, 10)). The city was politically, economically, and religiously important.

Its political prominence came from its being the capital of proconsular Asia. Its economic clout derived from its position as a large port city on major trade routes and as being the financial treasury for the East. Its religious leadership came from being a center for the worship of the pagan goddess Diana (Roman name), or Artemis.

The city was world famous for its magnificent temple. The Ephesians worshiped the Asiatic goddess Diana whose temple was one of the Seven Wonders of the World. It measured 425 by 220 by 60 feet, about four times the size of the Parthenon in Athens. It housed a statue of Diana, probably partially made from a fallen meteorite which gave rise to the legend that she had fallen down from Heaven. In the temple were deposits of huge amounts of treasure. It virtually served as the bank of Asia. Hundreds of priestesses (temple prostitutes) served the goddess in the temple. After the temple was destroyed by fire (356 B.C.) it was immediately rebuilt. However, after Paul's day it was destroyed in wars.

Three important roads met at Ephesus. One brought trade from the east via Colosse and Laodicea. One came from Galatia via Sardis and brought trade from Asia Minor. The third important road was to the north. This system of roads, coupled with the excellent seaport, made Ephesus the fourth greatest city in the Roman Empire (after Rome, Alexandria, and Antioch) with an estimated population of nearly 300,000.

THE ORIGIN OF THE CHURCH AT EPHESUS

When Paul was on his second preaching journey, he was "forbidden by the Holy Spirit to preach the word in Asia" (Acts 16:6). For some reason unknown to us,

Introduction

the door of opportunity for the preaching of the gospel in Asia was not yet open. The opening was in Europe, and Paul was guided there by the Holy Spirit. On returning from Europe in about A.D. 53, Paul, along with his faithful helpers, Aquila and Priscilla, visited Ephesus (Acts 18:18-21). As was his custom, Paul "entered the synagogue and reasoned with the Jews" (v. 19), but nothing is said about anyone obeying the gospel. Nevertheless, they wanted Paul to stay a longer time with them, but, pressed for time, he was not able to do so (v. 20), although he did promise to return to them, God willing (v. 21).

The Scriptures inform us that Aquila and Priscilla stayed behind in Ephesus (vv. 18,19). They were the church at Ephesus. Some time after Paul's departure, Apollos visited the city (Acts 18:24-28). Described as an "eloquent man and mighty in the Scriptures," Apollos was an Alexandrian Jew who had been "instructed in the way of the Lord," but "knew only the baptism of John" (v. 25). As his knowledge was imperfect, Priscilla and Aquila, upon hearing him speak publicly, "took him aside privately and explained to him the way of God more accurately" (v. 26). After this, Apollos desired to cross over to Achaia and "the brethren [at Ephesus] wrote, exhorting the disciples to receive him" (v. 27). The use of "the brethren" indicates there are others at Ephesus who were Christians besides Aquila and Priscilla. Who these other Christians are, we are not told. The church was probably still quite small and may possibly have been meeting in the home of Aquila and Priscilla.

In A.D. 54, after beginning his third preaching journey, Paul returned to Ephesus. While there, he discovers some disciples who had not yet been baptized into Christ. After these twelve obeyed the gospel, they no doubt sought to join themselves to the local church and were received with great rejoicing. Paul then went into the synagogue and spoke boldly for three months, "reasoning and persuading concerning the things of the kingdom of God" (Acts 19:7). When strong opposition to his teaching arose, he withdrew with the other Christians to the school of Tyrannus. There he continued daily to teach the gospel for two years (Acts 19:10).

Altogether, Paul spent three years at Ephesus with great success (Acts 20:31). Its excellent location was ideally suited for the spread of the gospel. Consequently, within the three years that Paul remained at Ephesus, the "word of the Lord" radiated throughout the whole province (Acts 19:10). This was no doubt accomplished in part through the fact of the great number of people who, for one reason or another, passed through the city, heard the gospel, and then carried it back to their homes located throughout Asia.

Ephesus and Asia were full of superstition, magic, charms, and all the other works of the occult. God, therefore, permitted "unusual miracles by the hands of Paul, so that even handkerchiefs or aprons were brought from his body to the sick, and the diseases left them and the evil spirits went out of them" (Acts 19:11,12). Furthermore, certain Jews who attempted to use as a charm the name of Jesus were utterly confounded by the evil spirits they tried to exorcise (Acts 19:13-16). As a result of all this, "the name of the Lord was magnified. And many who had believed

Introduction

came confessing and telling their deeds. Also, many of those who had practiced magic brought their books together and burned them in the sight of all.... So that the word of the Lord grew mightily and prevailed" (Acts 19:17b-20).

Timothy and Erastus also spent some time with Paul in Ephesus, but he eventually sent them on into Macedonia (Acts 19:22). As soon as he did this, there arose a great commotion over Diana of the Ephesians.

If the words of Demetrius are to be believed, she was worshipped by "all Asia and the world" (Acts 19:27). As a result, Paul's travel companions, Gaius and Aristarchus of Macedonia, were dragged into the theater. It is clear from the Bible account that these men's lives were in danger. Paul, ever the courageous soldier of the Cross, wanted to enter the theater but was prevented from doing so by the disciples who rightly feared the worst for him and his two companions if he showed his face to this chaotic assembly of goddess worshippers. After Alexander was set forth by the Jews, apparently in an attempt to defend the Jews from any association with *renegade* Jews (i.e., Christians) like "this fellow Paul" whom Gaius and Aristarchus abetted, pure pandemonium broke out for about two hours as the "disorderly gathering" cried out, "Great is Diana of the Ephesians" (Acts 19:34). Eventually, the city clerk was able to bring order to the theater and dismiss the crowd. After this, Paul called the disciples together, embraced them, and departed for Macedonia (Acts 20:1). He sailed to Macedonia and then traveled to Greece where he stayed for three months. Then, he, with his eight travel companions (Sopater, Aristarchus,

Secundus, Gaius, Timothy, Tychicus, Trophimus, and Luke), returned to Asia via Macedonia, stopping over at Troas. Sailing on to Miletus, about thirty miles south of Ephesus, he called for and met with the elders of the Ephesian church (Acts 20:17-38).

Timothy, a native of Lystra, was probably converted on Paul's first preaching journey (Acts 14:6-23). By the time of Paul's second preaching journey, he was well spoken of by the brethren at Lystra and Iconium (Acts 16:1,2). As we have already mentioned, he was with Paul in Ephesus on the third preaching journey but was sent to Macedonia just prior to the disturbance over the goddess Diana (Acts 16:3; 19:21,22). After Paul's release from his first Roman imprisonment, he left Timothy at Ephesus (I Timothy 1:3). While in Ephesus, Timothy received the epistles known to us as First Timothy and Second Timothy. A letter to the church at Ephesus is included in the book of Revelation (Revelation 2:1-7). All early church tradition claims that the apostle John lived here for two decades, from about A.D. 70 until his death.

OUTLINE

A traditional way of outlining the book is as follows:

Introduction—1:1-2

I. DOCTRINE: OUR SUFFICIENCY - Chapters 1 - 3

Key verse – 1:3 - "Blessed be the God and Father of our Lord Jesus Christ, who has blessed us with every spiritual blessing in the heavenly places in Christ.
Key Word—"blessings"

Introduction

A. What we have as a Possession – 1:4-14

B. What we need in Prayer – 1:15-23 – Enlightenment

C. What we hold as a Position – 2:1-22

    1. Raised and seated on the throne – 2:1-10
    2. Reconciled and set into the temple -- 2:11-22

D. What we need in Prayer 3:1-21 – Enablement

II. DUTY: OUR SUCCESS - Chapters 4 - 6

Key verse – 4:1 – "Therefore, the prisoner of the Lord, beseech you to have a walk worthy of the calling with which you were called.

Key word—"walk"

A. Walk in Unity—4:1-16

B. Walk in Purity—4:17—5:17

C. Walk in Light—4:17-32

D. Walk in Love—5:1-6

E. Walk as Children of Light—5:7-14

F. Walk in Submission—5:15-6:9

    1. To the Spirit 5:15-20

    2. To One Another 5:21-6:9
           a. Wives to husbands 5:22-24
           b. Husbands to wives 5:25-33

      c. Children to parents 6:1-4
      d. Servants to masters 6:5-8
      e. Masters to servants 6:9

G. Walk in Victory—6:10-24

Ephesians is one of those books which, like the God of whom it speaks, is beyond the grasp of the finite minds of men. "For now we see in a mirror dimly, but then face to face; now I know in part, but then I shall know fully just as I also have been fully known" (1 Cor.13:12). It is not that Ephesians is unclear, but that the truth of which it speaks is beyond our grasp. We should not be frustrated by the fact that we may not be able to "master" this epistle, but we should be humbled by the vastness of God's being, and of the finiteness of our own existence and intelligence.

KEY WORDS OR PHRASES USED IN EPHESIANS

"Riches"	5 times.
"Grace"	12 times.
"Glory"	8 times.
"Fullness, filled up, or fills"	6 times.
"In Christ (or in Him)"	15 times.

CHAPTER ONE
Redemption and Adoption

Greeting —1:1, 2

(1) Paul, an apostle of Jesus Christ by the will of God, To the saints who are in Ephesus, and faithful in Christ Jesus: (2) Grace to you and peace from God our Father and the Lord Jesus Christ.

1. **Paul**. It was the custom at this time to place the name of the writer at the beginning of a letter. **An apostle of Jesus Christ**. This was not just someone who thought he had something to say. No, indeed, this Paul is an apostle of Jesus Christ, and this is to be understood in the fullest meaning of the term *apostle*. He received his office directly from Christ. The marks of an apostle were abundantly evident in his life and work. He belongs to Christ, and represents Him. Therefore, Paul's message is Christ's own message. **By the will of God**. Paul is emphasizing the fact that his apostleship was not attained through aspiration, usurpation, nor nomination by other men. He was, instead, an apostle by divine preparation, having been set apart and qualified by the activity of God's sovereign will. **To the saints at Ephesus**. All Christians were called saints in the early church. The saints are those the Lord set apart to glorify Him. They are His *chosen generation*, His *royal priesthood*, His *holy nation*, His *own special people*, to proclaim His excellencies (I Peter 2:9). **And faithful in Christ Jesus**. This is not another group.

The saints and faithful form one unit. This is shown in the original in that the definite article is not repeated before the second word. The faithful saints at Ephesus are "in Christ Jesus," that is, they are what they are by virtue of their union with Christ. Without doubt, this expression is the most important one in this letter. It or its equivalent ("in Him," "in whom," "in the Beloved") or near-equivalent ("in the Lord") occurs in 1:1, 3, 4, 6, 7, 9-13, 15, 20; 2:5-7, 10, 13, 21, 22; 3:6, 11, 12, 21; 4:1, 21, 32; 5:8; and 6:10. It is in connection with Christ that they receive "every spiritual blessing" (1:3); *election* before the foundation of the world (1:4-6), *redemption* through His blood (1:7-12), and *certification* ("sealing") by the Holy Spirit as sons and therefore heirs (1:13,14).

2. **Grace to you and peace from God our Father and the Lord Jesus Christ**. This is the standard New Testament salutation. It is a prayer that God the Father and our Lord Jesus Christ may bestow favor and peace upon the Ephesian Christians. The Father is the source and the Lord is the mediator and procurer of these blessings. It should also be clear that the apostle Paul was not a Unitarian or "oneness" Pentecostal.

Redemption In Christ—1:3 – 14

> (3) Blessed {be} the God and Father of our Lord Jesus Christ, who has blessed us with every spiritual blessing in the heavenly {places} in Christ, (4) just as He chose us in Him before the foundation of the world, that we should be holy and without blame before Him in love, (5) having predestined us to adoption as sons by

Chapter One: Redemption and Adoption

Jesus Christ to Himself, according to the good pleasure of His will, (6) to the praise of the glory of His grace, by which He has made us accepted in the Beloved. (7) In Him we have redemption through His blood, the forgiveness of sins, according to the riches of His grace (8) which He made to abound toward us in all wisdom and prudence, (9) having made known to us the mystery of His will, according to His good pleasure which He purposed in Himself, (10) that in the dispensation of the fullness of the times He might gather together in one all things in Christ, both which are in heaven and which are on earth—in Him, (11) in whom also we have obtained an inheritance, being predestined according to the purpose of Him who works all things according to the counsel of His will, (12) that we who first trusted in Christ should be to the praise of His glory. (13) In Him you also {trusted}, after you heard the word of truth, the gospel of your salvation; in whom also, having believed, you were sealed with the Holy Spirit of promise, (14) who is the guarantee of our inheritance until the redemption of the purchased possession, to the praise of His glory.

3. **Blessed be the God and Father of our Lord Jesus Christ**. The Greek word rendered "blessed" is *eulogetos* and gives us our modern word *eulogize*. It means to bestow high praises upon. Therefore, Paul is eulogizing ("Praise be...") God for His marvelous blessings to the church. **Who has blessed us with every spiritual blessing in the heavenly places in Christ**. God the Father has not held back a single blessing from the church. The *heavenly places* here is

where God dwells. In other words, God blessed us in the heavens above; therefore, these blessings are infinitely superior to anything here on the earth below. All the blessings Paul will enumerate in this letter derives from these "heavenlies," the most notable being the very next blessing—God's eternal *choosing* or *election* of the faithful saints *in* (i.e., in connection with) His Son Jesus Christ.

4. **Just as He chose us in Him before the foundation of the world**. Before the foundation of the world, that is, in eternity before God created the universe (i.e., while He was "in the heavenly places"), the "God and Father of our Lord Jesus Christ," elected, selected, picked out, or chose (for this is the meaning of the Greek word *eklegomai*) "us" *in* Christ Jesus. This, of course, does not rule out the activities of the Son and Holy Spirit, but it does show that it was the Father who took the lead in the scheme of redemption. The "us" here are the faithful saints of verse 1, including Paul, and, by extension, all who at one time or another are *predestined* to become faithful saints. Contrary to what some think, the teaching of predestination is a Biblical subject. We will have more to say about this when we look at verse 5, but before we do so, we must learn the purpose of election. **That we should be holy and without blame before Him in love**. In other words, God, in His infinite wisdom, chose or elected those who would, *through* Christ, be holy and without blame before Him. This wonderful relationship between Redeemer and the redeemed would be one of mutual love.

Chapter One: Redemption and Adoption

5. Having predestined us to adoption as sons by Jesus to Himself, according to the good pleasure of His will. In connection with His having chosen before the foundation of the world those who would, through their relationship with Christ, be holy and blameless before Him, He is said to have *predestined* or *foreordained* certain ones ("we") who would be faithful saints to adoption as sons. But, how did He do this? He did it, the Scriptures tell us, by exercising His omniscience, particularly His foreknowledge (Romans 8:29,30; I Peter 1:2). Furthermore, the death of Jesus involved a similar combination of foreknowledge and predestination (Acts 2:23). Because God foreknew certain free will choices of men like Judas and Pilate, He could predestinate (arrange in advance) the death of Jesus Christ on the cross of Calvary. Thus, we conclude that God foreknows the future, even the contingent free will choices of human beings, and, therefore, can know not just the group of the saved generally (i.e., the corporate body or church), but the specific individuals who make up the church. This choosing and predestinating on God's behalf is not of individuals unconditionally. Instead, God's foreknowledge has permitted Him to select before the foundation of the world those who, of their own free will, would respond to God's grace in a positive way and allow themselves to be "conformed to the image of His Son" (Romans 8:29). In other words, these verses are speaking of the *election* and *predestination* of individuals conditioned upon God's foreknowledge of their obedience to the gospel (cf. II Thessalonians 2:13-17).

6. To the praise of the glory of His grace, by which He has made us accepted in the Beloved. Those who are adopted as sons are to manifest praise and honor to the wonderful and magnificent glory of God's amazing grace. They are, as a result of such grace, acceptable to the Father *only* in their connection with Christ, who is the Beloved of the Father (cf. Colossians 1:13). Since Christ, by means of His death, earned every spiritual blessing for us, and therefore wants us to have these things, and since the Father loves the Son, it is only reasonable to believe that, for the sake of this beloved One, the Father will gladly grant unto us everything we need. In fact, the Father Himself gave His Son for this very purpose. Hence, "He who did not spare His own Son, but delivered Him up for us all, how shall He not with Him also freely give us all things?" (Romans 8:32).

7. **In Him we have redemption through His blood, the forgiveness of sins, according to the riches of His grace**. In Him, that is to say, the Beloved, we have *redemption*. This word, as in Colossians 1:14, indicates *deliverance as a result of the payment of a ransom*. We who were in bondage to sin have been set free by God's grace through our connection with the blood of Christ. Although the Beloved did many wonderful things while He was in this world, for example, he stilled the tempest, cast our demons, cleansed the lepers, opened the eyes of the blind, unstopped the ears of the deaf, fed the hungry, healed the sick, and even raised the dead, His ultimate mission was to seek and save the lost, to give Himself a ransom for many (Isaiah 53:12; Matthew 20:28; Mark 10:45; Luke 19:10; I Timothy 1:15). As we contemplate this wonderful sacrifice, we join with the four living creatures and the twenty-four elders who are forever exclaiming, "You are worthy...for You were slain, and have redeemed us to

God by Your blood" (Revelation 5:9), and the ten thousand times ten thousand and thousands of thousands of angels lifting up their voices in enthusiastic worship, shouting, "Worthy is the Lamb who has been slain...to receive honor and glory and blessing!" (Revelation 5:12).

8. **Which He made to abound toward us in all wisdom and prudence**. God's grace is still under discussion. He causes it to abound or overflow in our direction. In a similar passage, Paul wrote, "And the grace of our Lord was exceedingly abundant, with faith and love which are in Christ" (I Timothy 1:14). Consequently, as God's wonderful grace abounds toward us, it not only provokes *faith* and *love* in Christ, but it also produces *wisdom* and *prudence* in the faithful saint. A parallel to this is found in Colossians 1:9, which reads, "For this reason we also, since the day we heard it, do not cease to pray for you, and to ask that you may be filled with the knowledge of His will in all wisdom and spiritual understanding." Wisdom, of course, is *knowledge plus*. It is the ability to apply knowledge to the best advantage. Prudence, or spiritual understanding, is *penetrating insight* into what is true from God's standpoint.

9. **Having made known to us the mystery of His will**. All this wisdom and spiritual insight comes from God's revealing to us the "mystery of His will," which, according to verse 10, was God's eternal purpose to gather together in one all things *in Christ*. **According to His good pleasure, which He purposed in Himself**. In verse 5, we were told that we were predestined "according to the good pleasure" of the Father's will. Again, we learn that in eternity it was the Father's good pleasure to set forth His plan to redeem

fallen mankind through His only begotten Son, Jesus Christ.

10. **That in the dispensation of the fullness of the times.** In the Father's eternal plan, there was a specific period of time when He would send forth His Son, "born of a woman, born under the law, to redeem those who were under the law, that we might receive the adoption of sons" (Galatians 4:4,5). Here, and in verse 10, as in other places, the expression "fullness of times" or "last days" is often applied to the period of Christ's first coming (cf. Hebrews 1:2; I Peter 1:20). All the previous time periods reached their fullness when this dispensation (the Christian era) began. More specifically, ever since the death, burial, resurrection, and coronation of Jesus Christ, this dispensation of the fullness of times has been in effect. It will not end until the Lord returns and has executed judgment (I Corinthians 15:24,25). **He might gather together in one all things in Christ, both which are in heaven and which are on earth.** The plan was that all things would come under the authority of "the Christ of God." Consequently, the resurrected Lord said *all authority* was given Him in heaven and earth (Matthew 28:18). And in Philippians 2:9-11, we learn that Christ Jesus has been given a "name which is above every name, that at the name of Jesus every knee should bow, of those in heaven, and of those on earth, and of those under the earth, and that every tongue should confess that Jesus Christ is Lord, to the glory of God the Father." —**Him**. That is, Jesus Christ, King of kings and Lord of lords.

11. **In whom also we have obtained an inheritance**. Note the word *also*, meaning: *not only* did we, in

Chapter One: Redemption and Adoption

connection with Christ, receive such blessings as redemption, forgiveness of sins, and spiritual understanding (wisdom and prudence), benefits which have already been mentioned (vv. 7-10), but, in addition to these (which, although they have *lasting* significance, focus attention on *the past*) we have graciously been made heirs, which in turn causes us to look forward to *future* glory. This "inheritance" is spelled out in its fullness in Romans 8:30, "Moreover whom He predestined, these He also called; whom He called, these He also justified; and whom He justified, these He also glorified." It consists of two stages: certain blessings are bestowed upon us in the here and now, and others in the hereafter (cf. vv. 13 and 14 below). **Being predestined according to the purpose of Him who works all things according to the counsel of His will**. Man's salvation *in Christ* originated with our Heavenly Father, and flows totally from His grace. Therefore, He predestined (determined beforehand) that He would adopt us as sons *by Jesus Christ* (v. 5).

12. **That we who first trusted in Christ should be to the praise of His glory**. The hope or trust that Christians have *in Christ* is to the praise of the Father's glory, specifically, His marvelous grace. There does not seem to be any reason to contrast the "we" in this verse with the "you" in the next verse, as if Paul were writing of two different groups. From verse 3, he has used "we" and "us" to refer to all the Ephesian Christians, plus himself, and by extension, any faithful saint. Consequently, in verse 13, he is addressing the Ephesians more directly, who had heard the gospel from him.

13. **In Him you also trusted, after you heard the word of truth, the gospel of your salvation**. As was pointed out in our commentary on the previous verse, the Ephesians had heard "the word of truth, the gospel of [their] salvation" from Paul himself. It was, therefore, appropriate for him to switch to "you" as he directed his words to them. **In whom also, having believed, you were sealed with the Holy Spirit of promise**. All faithful saints, by their connection with Jesus Christ, are "sealed with the Holy Spirit of promise," which took place when they were baptized into Christ (cf. Acts 2:38 and 5:32; II Corinthians 1:22). The *seal* under consideration here does not refer to the sealing away of something in a container for the purpose of preservation; it refers, instead, to the seal or "stamp of ownership" used by the ancients to validate something. The Jew considered circumcision as God's stamp of ownership on him. Here Paul identifies the "gift of the Holy Spirit" received in baptism (Acts 2:38) with the "circumcision of Christ" (cf. Colossians 2:11-13).

14. **Who is the guarantee of our inheritance until the redemption of the purchased possession**. The indwelling of the Holy Spirit that each Christian receives (cf. John 7:37-39; Acts 2:38 and 5:32; II Corinthians 1:22 and 5:5) is the "pledge money" or "down payment" that assures us that we will receive the full payment of our completed redemption in due time. This redemption, which is described as an "adoption as sons" (v. 5), is, of course, "in Christ" (v. 3). Consequently, it is "through His blood" that we receive the "forgiveness of sins" (v. 7). But, and this is the point of this verse, this forgiveness of sins that we receive through the blood of Christ in baptism is only

Chapter One: Redemption and Adoption

the beginning of a *process* (cf. Romans 8:29,30) that will eventually culminate in the redemption of our bodies (Romans 8:23; Philippians 3:20,21). **To the praise of His glory**. All this, which is the result of God's grace toward us, is to the praise of His glory.

Prayer For Spiritual Wisdom—1:15 – 23

> (15) Therefore I also, after I heard of your faith in the Lord Jesus and your love for all the saints, (16) do not cease to give thanks for you, making mention of you in my prayers: (17) that the God of our Lord Jesus Christ, the Father of glory, may give to you the spirit of wisdom and revelation in the knowledge of Him, (18) the eyes of your understanding being enlightened; that you may know what is the hope of His calling, what are the riches of the glory of His inheritance in the saints, (19) and what {is} the exceeding greatness of His power toward us who believe, according to the working of His mighty power (20) which He worked in Christ when He raised Him from the dead and seated {Him} at His right hand in the heavenly {places}, (21) far above all principality and power and might and dominion, and every name that is named, not only in this age but also in that which is to come. (22) And He put all {things} under His feet, and gave Him {to be} head over all {things} to the church, (23) which is His body, the fullness of Him who fills all in all.

15. **Therefore I also, after I heard of your faith in the Lord Jesus and your love for all the saints**. It has been four or five years since Paul has been with these brethren personally, but he continues to hear of

their *enduring* faith in the Lord and its subsequent result—their love for all the saints. The fact that he starts this with the expression "I also" indicates there were others, probably those who were then with him, who were also thankful for the Ephesians' faith and love.

16. **Do not cease to give thanks for you, making mention of you in my prayers**. The blossoming of the gospel among the Ephesians gave the imprisoned Paul reason to thank God. It was he who had planted the gospel at Ephesus and he prayed for them on a regular basis. As for his prayers for others, see Romans 1:9; Philippians 1:4; Colossians 1:9; I Thessalonians 1:2; II Thessalonians 1:11; and Philemon 4.

17. **That the God of our Lord Jesus Christ, the Father of glory, may give to you the spirit of wisdom and revelation in the knowledge of Him**. Paul's prayer of thanksgiving flows over into intercession. He prays to the glorious God and Father of the Lord Jesus Christ that they would have a spirit that is rich in the wisdom that is derived from God's revelation, the gospel of Jesus Christ (cf. Colossians 1:9). Paul wants the Ephesians to really know God, the Father of glory, as a result of the things He *has done*, *is doing*, and *will do* for them in connection with His only begotten Son, Jesus Christ.

18. **The eyes of your understanding being enlightened; that you may know what is the hope of His calling**. The KJV reads "eyes of your heart." The *heart*, as it is here used, means the innermost center of man. It is the seat of the *understanding* and

Chapter One: Redemption and Adoption

the source of thoughts, desires, emotions, words, and actions. Whatever is in the heart rules the conduct. Paul wants these Ephesians to understand in their hearts and minds the grandeur and wealth of their blessings in Christ. He wants them to understand all the wonderful significance of "hope" they have as a result of being "called" by the Father through the gospel of Christ (cf. II Thessalonians 2:14). The Father will deliver us from this present world and will richly supply us "an entrance...into the everlasting kingdom of our Lord and Savior Jesus Christ" (II Peter 1:11). This *hope* we have is "an anchor of the soul, both sure and steadfast" (Hebrews 6:19). Of this hope Paul wrote: "But indeed I also count all things loss for the excellence of the knowledge of Christ Jesus my Lord, for whom I have suffered the loss of all things, and count them as rubbish, that I may gain Christ and be found in Him, not having my own righteousness, which is from the law, but that which is through faith in Christ, the righteousness which is from God by faith; that I may know Him and the power of His resurrection, and the fellowship of His sufferings, being conformed to His death, if, by any means, I may attain to the resurrection from the dead. Not that I have already attained, or am already perfected; but I press on, that I may lay hold of that for which Christ Jesus has also laid hold of me. Brethren, I do not count myself to have apprehended; but one thing I do, forgetting those things which are behind and reaching forward to those things which are ahead, I press toward the goal for the prize of the upward call of God in Christ Jesus" (Philippians 3:8-14). **What are the riches of the glory of His inheritance in the saints**. All faithful saints generally, and here the Ephesians specifically, are "His inheritance" (v. 11). How could this be other than rich in glory (cf. I Corinthians 2:9)?

19. **And what is the exceeding greatness of His power toward us who believe, according to the working of His mighty power**. All this derives from and continues to depend upon the Almighty God.

20. **Which He worked in Christ when He raised Him from the dead and seated Him at His right hand in the heavenly places**. This, too, is the result of the Father's almighty power, and, therefore, proof positive that He will one day complete the redemption we have in Christ when He will raise our bodies from the dead and glorify us as He did His Son.

21. **Far above all principality and power and might and dominion, and every name that is named, not only in this age but also in that which is to come**. Jesus is "Lord of lords and King of kings" (Revelation 17:14). The only one excepted from His authority is the Father who gave it to Him (I Corinthians 15:27). Christ's lordship is universal and it shall never be eclipsed in this world or in eternity.

22. **And He put all things under His feet, and gave Him to be head over all things to the church**. "All things" (i.e., *everything*) is under the ultimate authority and control of Christ. Therefore, it should not surprise us that Christ is also head over all things to the church, the called out body of the redeemed, "which He purchased with His own blood" (Acts 20:28). This body receives its instructions, its life, and its strength from Jesus Christ.

23. **Which is His body, the fullness of Him who fills all in all**. The church (i.e., the called out ones) is/are the body of Christ. See also Colossians 1:18, where this order is reversed. There is only one called

out body and this is the church of (or in connection with) Christ (cf. Ephesians 4:4). Christ, "who is the fullness of Him who fills all in all" (cf. Colossians 2:9), is given to the church, which in other places is called His "bride," by the Father. In fact, in chapter five of this book, the relationship between a husband and wife is related to the relationship between Christ and His church. Indeed, what marvelous and magnificent blessings are ours in Christ Jesus our Lord.

CHAPTER TWO
Grace Through Faith

Salvation By Grace Through Faith—2:1 – 10

(1) And you {He made alive}, who were dead in trespasses and sins, (2) in which you once walked according to the course of this world, according to the prince of the power of the air, the spirit who now works in the sons of disobedience, (3) among whom also we all once conducted ourselves in the lusts of our flesh, fulfilling the desires of the flesh and of the mind, and were by nature children of wrath, just as the others. (4) But God, who is rich in mercy, because of His great love with which He loved us, (5) even when we were dead in trespasses, made us alive together with Christ (by grace you have been saved), (6) and raised {us} up together, and made {us} sit together in the heavenly {places} in Christ Jesus, (7) that in the ages to come He might show the exceeding riches of His grace in {His} kindness toward us in Christ Jesus. (8) For by grace you have been saved through faith, and that not of yourselves; {it is} the gift of God, (9) not of works, lest anyone should boast. (10) For we are His workmanship, created in Christ Jesus for good works, which God prepared beforehand that we should walk in them.

1. **And you He made alive, who were dead in trespasses and sins**. With the starting of this new chapter, there is a transition in thought. Paul, who has

been praising God and thanking Him for the faith of the Ephesians, and praying for their continued enlightenment, now begins to remind them of what they once were and what they now are in Christ. In the past, these Ephesians, although they knew the mysteries and secrets involved in their paganism, were spiritually dead in their disobedience and sins. They have now been "quickened" or made alive (cf. Colossians 2:13).

2. In which you once walked according to the course of this world, according to the prince of the power of the air, the spirit who now works in the sons of disobedience. These Ephesians, both Jews and Gentiles, had once been among the "living dead" (I Timothy 5:6), who are ruled by satan, "the prince of the power of the air." In other words, when we "walk" or conduct our lives in a worldly fashion (i.e., with no consideration of what God has to say) we are allowing ourselves to be controlled by the devil. God works in His sons "both to will and to do for His good pleasure" (Philippians 2:13). Satan, too, works in his children (cf. John 8:42-44).

3. Among whom also we all once conducted ourselves in the lusts of our flesh, fulfilling the desires of the flesh, and of the mind, and were by nature children of wrath, just as the others. Paul makes it clear that the matter of disobedience and sin is a universal problem. None have been immune. We were all in the same condition. We were all part of that group that we now understand is made up of the "living dead." At one time, "all" Christians, just like everyone else, walked according to the *lusts* and *desires* of the "flesh" (which is used here by Paul in its negative sense) and our debased minds. According to

Galatians 5:19-21, some of these are: "adultery, fornication, uncleanness, licentiousness, idolatry, sorcery, hatred, contentions, jealousies, outbursts of wrath, selfish ambitions, dissensions, heresies, envy, murders, drunkenness, revelries, and the like...." In this condition, our natures were corrupted by disobedience and sin and we were doomed to suffer God's wrath.

4. **But, God, who is rich in mercy, because of His great love with which He loved us**. The picture of the preceding verses is one of ruin and judgment; nevertheless, the *but* here is quite emphatic, and totally reverses this very bleak picture. God hates sin and disobedience but is abundant in His mercy toward the sinner. And if mercy is His attitude towards us, and it most certainly is, then surely it is His great love for us that serves as His motive for all He does for us in Christ. And, as we have already learned, this great love began with God in eternity and is the reason "He chose us in Him before the foundation of the world" (1:4), "having predestined us to adoption as sons by Jesus Christ to Himself, according to the good pleasure of His will" (1:5).

5. **Even when we were dead in trespasses, made us alive together with Christ**. The process of ruin has now been reversed. We are no longer the "living dead." Instead, we have been "born again" (John 3:7), "raised from the dead...[to] walk in newness of life" (Romans 6:4), or "made alive...together with Christ," "having forgiven [us] all [our] trespasses" (Colossians 2:13). **(By grace you have been saved)**. God acted toward us (the world) in mercy motivated by love when we were in spiritually dead. Consequently, this

Chapter Two: Grace Through Faith

salvation we now enjoy in Christ is the result of God's grace or unmerited favor toward us.

6. **And raised us up together, and made us sit together in the heavenly places in Christ Jesus**. Just as the omnipotence of God raised up Christ alive, it also raises us up spiritually to "a newness of life" (Romans 6:4). Christ, of course, was not just raised up alive, but He was also exalted "at His [the Father's] right hand in the heavenly places" (1:20). In 1:3 and 1:20, "the heavenly places" clearly refers to the heaven of God's glory, the dwelling place of God Himself. Here, in this verse, "the heavenly places in Christ" refer to the church, the kingdom of God on earth. Speaking of this spiritual kingdom when He stood before Pilate, Jesus said: "My kingdom is not of this world. If My kingdom were of this world, My servants would fight, so that I should not be delivered to the Jews" (John 18:36). Christians have been raised up to reign together with Christ in His church, the kingdom of God on earth. Quite appropriately Christians are referred to elsewhere as "kings and priests" or, literally, "a kingdom of priests" (Revelation 1:6). In 6:12, Paul uses "the heavenly places" to refer to the supermundane or spiritual domain of demonic forces who array themselves against us. This expression then has at least three different meanings and is best determined by the context in which it is used.

7. **That in the ages to come He might show the exceeding riches of His grace in His kindness toward us in Christ Jesus**. The "ages to come" is eternity. In eternity God is going to make such a spectacle of His grace and kindness toward the

redeemed in Christ that all the heavenly hosts and saints will glorify Him.

8. **For by grace you have been saved through faith, and that not of yourselves; it is the gift of God**. If they were Jews, these Ephesians had not been saved by their perfect keeping of the Law of Moses, and if they were Gentiles, they were not saved because of what they had learned through their mystery religions. They were saved by grace (this is God's part) through faith (this is their part). The "gift" is salvation, not faith. If God, because of His love, kindness, mercy, and grace, had not initiated His eternal scheme of redemption, there is no way man could be saved. Faith, of course, comes by hearing and believing God's Word (Romans 10:17). Therefore, salvation, a gift of God, is something to be *seized* rather than *achieved*. Furthermore, and one must never lose sight of this fact, faith, truth faith, the kind of faith under discussion in this verse, is more than just believing (James 2:19).

9. **Not of works, lest anyone should boast**. Again, their salvation, which was a gift from God, did not come by the works of the Law, nor by any works of man's invention or device. Salvation was not bestowed by God as a result of their efforts, therefore there was nothing for them to boast about. It is absolutely unconscionable for anyone to use what Paul is here writing as an excuse for teaching that man cannot and must not do anything in order to be saved, because, if he did, it would not be totally of God's grace. There are the works of men in which, before God, no man can glory, and there are the works "of God" which all men are obligated to do by

faith (John 6:29). In other words, our faith obligates us to obey (cf. James 2:14-26).

10. **For we are His workmanship, created in Christ Jesus for good works, which God prepared beforehand that we should walk in them**. The church of Christ is the workmanship of God, and we were "created in Christ Jesus for good works." These works "of God" were determined "beforehand" in the mind of God, and it is for the doing of these works that we were *created*. As God, through His omnipotence, created Adam, so He creates us spiritually in Christ. Again, "in Christ" tells where this creation takes place. It is in our connection with Christ: "Therefore, if anyone is in Christ, he is a new creation; old things have passed away; behold, all things have become new" (II Corinthians 5:17). Consequently, we are told to not just be *hearers*, but *doers* of the "work" also (James 1:25).

Brought Near By The Blood Of Christ—2:11 – 13

> (11) Therefore remember that you, once Gentiles in the flesh — who are called Uncircumcision by what is called the Circumcision made in the flesh by hands — (12) that at that time you were without Christ, being aliens from the commonwealth of Israel and strangers from the covenants of promise, having no hope and without God in the world. (13) But now in Christ Jesus you who once were far off have been made near by the blood of Christ.

11. **Therefore remember that you, once Gentiles in the flesh—who are called Uncircumcision by what**

is called the Circumcision made in the flesh by hands—. "You" and "we" have been used freely up to this point. As has already been said, some of the Ephesians were Jewish, but most were Gentiles. Thus far, Paul has not used these pronouns to distinguish between Jew and Gentile, but here he makes a distinction. He now uses "you" to specifically refer to the Gentile Christians. Nevertheless, there are two groups in the church at Ephesus: the Uncircumcision (the Gentiles) and the Circumcision (the Jews). In their previous condition, neither of these groups were right with God. Notice that the Jews had been circumcised *in the flesh* not *in their hearts*.

12. **That at that time you were without Christ, being aliens from the commonwealth of Israel and strangers from the covenants of promise, having no hope and without God in the world**. The former condition of these Gentiles was totally reprehensible. They knew nothing about Christ. They had never had the advantage of being citizens of the commonwealth of Israel and were completely ignorant of the promises and covenants God had made with Abraham (Genesis 12:2,3). They were without God and had absolutely no hope of ever getting out of this world alive. The five-fold negative description of this verse has a cumulative effect. The situation grows worse and worse with the last clause, "and without God in the world," as the climax.

13. **But now in Christ Jesus you who once were far off have been made near by the blood of Christ**. But now, in Christ, these who had been so far from being what they ought to be, were now, by their

obedience to the gospel, made near by the blood of Christ. This was always God's intent. Saving the Gentiles was not an afterthought of God. When Jesus came into this world to seek and save that which was lost, He said: "As the Father knows Me, even so I know the Father; and I lay down my life for the sheep. And other sheep I have which are not of this fold: them also I must bring, and they will hear My voice; and there will be one flock and one shepherd" (John 10:15,16).

Christ Our Peace—2:14 – 18

> (14) For He Himself is our peace, who has made both one, and has broken down the middle wall of division {between us}, (15) having abolished in His flesh the enmity, {that is,} the law of commandments {contained} in ordinances, so as to create in Himself one new man {from} the two, {thus} making peace, (16) and that He might reconcile them both to God in one body through the cross, thereby putting to death the enmity.
>
> (17) And He came and preached peace to you who were afar off and to those who were near.
>
> (18) For through Him we both have access by one Spirit to the Father.

14. For He Himself is our peace. Jesus Christ, as a result of shedding His blood, is not just the peacemaker, but is "our peace," because in His person, as God-man, the reconciliation took place. Through Him there is peace between God and man and Jew and Gentile. This double meaning runs through this verse and the one following. This latter peace, the one he mentions in this verse, is actually made possible by the first. **Who has made both one**. Both Jew and Gentile are one in their connection with Christ. If they truly belong to Christ, they are unified. This is the only way Jew and Gentile will ever be one. **And has broken down the middle wall of division between us**. The wall of division between these two groups was the Law of Moses, with its ordinances and observances (cf. Acts 10:28), which kept the Jews separate from the Gentiles, much like the actual wall of division in the Jerusalem Temple beyond which a Gentile was not permitted to go.

15. **Having abolished in His flesh the enmity, that is, the law of commandments contained in ordinances**. Through His death, Jesus Christ abolished the Law (Colossians 2:14). In other words, we are no longer under a system of perfect lawkeeping for justification, but under grace (Romans 6:14). **So as to create in Himself one new man from the two, thus making peace**. The long feud between the human family is healed in Christ. There is now one fold and one shepherd. As Paul said in the Galatian letter: "There is neither Jew nor Greek, there is neither slave nor free, there is neither male nor female; for you are all one in Christ Jesus. And if you are Christ's, then you are Abraham's seed, and heirs according to the promise" (Galatians 3:28,29).

16. **And that He might reconcile them both to God in one body through the cross**. This is the reconciliation that Paul wrote about in II Corinthians 5:19, "that is, that God was in Christ reconciling the world to Himself, not imputing their trespasses to

them, and has committed to us the word of reconciliation." The word of reconciliation is the gospel, which, when obeyed, reconciles man to God *first*, and *then*, as Paul has pointed out in the previous verses, to other men, regardless of their race, sex, or social status (Galatians 3:28). This reconciliation is in the "one body" of 1:22,23 and Colossians 1:18, which could not have existed without the work of the cross. **Thereby putting to death the enmity**. How? "By His grace through the redemption that is in Christ, whom God set forth to be a propitiation by His blood, through faith, to demonstrate His righteousness, because in His forbearance God had passed over the sins that were previously committed, to demonstrate at the present time His righteousness, that He might be just and the justifier of the one who has faith in Jesus" (Romans 3:24-26). Through the cross of Christ, sin has been punished. Therefore, God is *just*. Through the cross of Christ, the penalty for our sins has been paid vicariously. Therefore, God can be the *justifier* of those who exercise faith in His Son.

17. **And He came and preached peace to you who were afar off and to those who were near**. This preaching was not the preaching that Christ had done personally, but was the preaching done by the apostles and other preachers of the gospel (cf. Hebrews 1:2). Both the Gentile and the Jew heard this preaching.

18. **For through Him we both have access by one Spirit to the Father**. In order to see the king, one had to be introduced by one close to him. Paul uses this symbolism to demonstrate that it is only *through* this "one Mediator,...the Man Jesus Christ" (I Timothy 2:5), that any of us, Jew or Gentile, have access to

the Father. However, this is not done without the work of the "one Spirit" (I Corinthians 12:13).

Christ Our Cornerstone—2:19 – 22

> (19) Now, therefore, you are no longer strangers and foreigners, but fellow citizens with the saints and members of the household of God, (20) having been built on the foundation of the apostles and prophets, Jesus Christ Himself being the chief {cornerstone}, (21) in whom the whole building, being joined together, grows into a holy temple in the Lord, (22) in whom you also are being built together for a habitation of God in the Spirit.

19. **Now, therefore, you are no longer strangers and foreigners, but fellow citizens with the saints and members of the household of God.** Being formed into one *sanctified household* (the house of God, family of God, or church of Christ) along with the Jews, the Gentiles were strangers and foreigners no longer.

20. **Having been built on the foundation of the apostles and prophets**. The household of God is a "spiritual house" constructed out of "living stones" (I Peter 2:5). The laying of this foundation was accomplished by the preaching of the gospel (cf. 3:5). **Jesus Christ Himself being the chief cornerstone**. The two parts of this spiritual house are held together by Jesus Christ Himself, the chief cornerstone.

21. **In whom the whole building, being joined together, grows into a holy temple in the Lord**. Jesus Christ does not just hold it together, but He also

causes it to grow into a sacred temple (I Corinthians 3:16) by bringing new members (converts) into the church.

22. **In whom you also are being built together for a habitation of God in the Spirit**. In their connection with Christ, both the Jewish and Gentile Christians in Ephesus were part of the universal body of Christ. In sum-total with all the other churches, they formed the invisible body of Christ, the church which He built (Matthew 16:18) and purchased with His own blood (Acts 20:28). "A habitation of God in the Spirit" is equivalent to "a holy temple in the Lord" in verse 21. God in the Spirit (i.e., Father, Son, and Holy Spirit) dwells in the church, His sacred temple (I Corinthians 3:16), a spiritual house not built with hands (Acts 7:48 and 17:24).

CHAPTER THREE
Glory and Praise

The Mystery Revealed—3:1 – 7

(1) For this reason I, Paul, the prisoner of Jesus Christ for you Gentiles — (2) if indeed you have heard of the dispensation of the grace of God which was given to me for you, (3) how that by revelation He made known to me the mystery (as I wrote before in a few words, (4) by which, when you read, you may understand my knowledge in the mystery of Christ), (5) which in other ages was not made known to the sons of men, as it has now been revealed by the Spirit to His holy apostles and prophets: (6) that the Gentiles should be fellow heirs, of the same body, and partakers of His promise in Christ through the gospel, (7) of which I became a minister according to the gift of the grace of God given to me by the effective working of His power.

1. **For this reason**. What he now writes is to be connected with what has already been written. **I, Paul, the prisoner of Jesus Christ for you Gentiles**—. Before Paul was in Christ, he used to put Christians in prison. Now, because he is an apostle to the Gentiles, he finds himself in prison. In fact, his chains authenticate his apostleship (II Corinthians 11:16-33). In every reference that Paul makes of himself as a prisoner, he stresses that he belongs to

Chapter Three: Glory and Praise

Jesus Christ, his Lord (4:1; Philemon 1:9; II Timothy 1:8).

2. **If indeed you have heard of the dispensation of the grace of God which was given to me for you**. This is a difficult construction. Is he questioning whether the Ephesians know of his part in proclaiming the gospel? Surely not! He knows some of them personally and knows they know his work as an apostle. The fact that five years have passed since he was with them would indicate that others had obeyed the gospel since then. It is, therefore, perfectly proper for him to say "if indeed you have heard."

3. **How that by revelation He made known to me the mystery**. Paul always insists that his apostleship to the Gentiles and his knowledge of the revealed mystery did not come from human origin (Galatians 1:12). **(As I wrote before in a few words**. Some think he is referring to a letter now lost. He is probably just referring to what he has just written in 2:11-22.

4. **By which, when you read, you may understand my knowledge in the mystery of Christ)**. Paul wrote to be understood. He did not use the loquacious rhetoric or "great swelling words of emptiness" (II Peter 2:18) of the Greek and Roman schools of oratory. When we read what Paul wrote, then we can know what he knew by divine revelation.

5. **Which in other ages was not made known to the sons of men, as it has now been revealed by the Spirit to His holy apostles and prophets:**. This "mystery of Christ" had never been fully revealed until it was made known to the holy apostles and prophets by the Holy Spirit (cf. John 14:26; I Corinthians 12:8).

6. That the Gentiles should be fellow heirs, of the same body, and partakers of His promise in Christ through the gospel. This is not to say that no one, not even prophets like Moses, Isaiah, etc., knew anything about the future blessing in which the Gentiles would share. In fact, the Old Testament writers did know about it and referred to it over and over (Gen 12:3; 22:18; 26:4; 28:14; Psalm 72; 87; Isaiah 11:10; 49:6; 54:1-3; 60:1-3; Hosea 1:10; Amos 9:11ff; Malachi 1:11; etc.). What they did not know was that the old theocracy would be abolished and in its place the church of Christ would be established and in this body the Gentiles and Jews would be on equal footing before God.

7. Of which I became a minister according to the gift of the grace of God given to me by the effective working of His power. The office with which Paul had been invested was a gift of God's grace. Verse 8 makes this even clearer. He became a Christian by obeying the gospel like everyone else; but he became an apostle and minister of the gospel by the power of God. God was working in and through Paul. Paul deserved none of the credit.

Purpose Of The Mystery—3:8 – 13

> (8) To me, who am less than the least of all the saints, this grace was given, that I should preach among the Gentiles the unsearchable riches of Christ, (9) and to make all {people} see what {is} the fellowship of the mystery, which from the beginning of the ages has been hidden in God who created all things through Jesus Christ; (10) to the intent that now the manifold wisdom of God might be made known

Chapter Three: Glory and Praise

by the church to the principalities and powers in the heavenly {places}, (11) according to the eternal purpose which He accomplished in Christ Jesus our Lord, (12) in whom we have boldness and access with confidence through faith in Him. (13) Therefore I ask that you do not lose heart at my tribulations for you, which is your glory.

8. **To me, who am less than the least of all the saints, this grace was given, that I should preach among the Gentiles**. Paul does not call himself the "least" but "less than the least" of all saints. This is not just false humility on his part. To think that a man with a record like Paul, a violent persecutor of the church, should upon his conversion be made one of the Lord's chosen apostles seems absolutely incredible. Nevertheless, it is true. We certainly would not have done this, but God did. "Gift," "given," and "was given" in this verse and in verse 7 glorify the magnificent Giver. Paul's office in the church of Christ was an almost unbelievable gift, and he never grew tired of saying so (cf. I Corinthians 15:9-11; I Timothy 1:15). **The unsearchable riches of Christ**. Some translate "unsearchable" as "unfathomable." The idea being something that cannot be *tracked* or *traced*. The same word is used in Romans 11:33. Man could have never understood the spiritual riches connected with Christ unless God Himself had revealed it.

9. **And to make all people see what is the fellowship of the mystery, which from the beginning of the ages has been hidden in God who created all things through Jesus Christ;**. This was the purpose of Paul's preaching to the Gentiles. Preaching the unsearchable riches of Christ was like

setting this mystery that had been hidden in the mind of God into the fullest light of day so that all men could see it clearly. In contrast with the pagan mystery religions which claimed to reveal secrets to the privileged few, Paul states that his mission is to tell *all people*. Of course, all men would not take advantage of the gospel, but the preaching of it would place the unsearchable riches before them to hear and see. That this was effectively done by Paul can be seen from the eloquent testimony of Demetruis, who rejected the gospel, in Acts 19:26.

10. **To the intent that now the manifold wisdom of God might be made known by the church to the principalities and powers in the heavenly places,.** Not in times past but *now,* the manifold or *infinite diversity* of God's wisdom is made known to the angelic rulers and powers. This is accomplished through what God has done *by means of* or *through* the church. The reconciliation of Jew and Gentile to God and to each other through the cross of Christ—which to the Jew is a stumbling block and to the Gentile foolishness (I Corinthians 1:22-25)—manifests the manifold wisdom of Almighty God. God's wisdom reconciles the irreconcilables! Therefore, it should not surprise us that the angelic hosts have learned a great deal about the God they adore by watching what He has done *through* or *by means of* the church. Angels have been curious about the things connected with man's redemption in Christ Jesus (I Peter 1:12), and are themselves "ministering spirits sent forth to minister for those who will inherit salvation" (Hebrews 1:14).

Chapter Three: Glory and Praise

11. According to the eternal purpose which He accomplished in Christ Jesus our Lord,. What "has been hidden in God" (v. 9) has "now" been "made known" (v. 10). God's "eternal purpose" to save mankind, which becomes visible in the church, was not some last minute thought on His part. The scheme of redemption in all of history is focused in and through Jesus Christ and His church.

12. In whom we have boldness and access with confidence through faith in Him. In our connection with Jesus Christ our Lord, we have the boldness (or *courage*) that lets us draw near to the throne of grace (Hebrews 4:16) and *confident access* to the Father (John 14:6) and all those spiritual blessings mentioned in 1:3. This courage and confident access stems directly from our faith (i.e., *trust* and *reliance*) in Jesus.

13. Therefore I ask that you do not lose heart at my tribulations for you, which is your glory. Paul does not want the Ephesians to be disheartened by the imprisonment, persecutions, and sufferings that he experienced preaching the gospel for their sake. In another letter written to those who were anxious about his imprisonment and tribulations, he had written that the things that happened to him had actually turned out for the furtherance of the gospel (Philippians 1:12). Knowing his labor for them and their spiritual blessings they have in connection with Jesus Christ, this great apostle to the Gentiles wants them to be both *bold* and *confident*. One might be tempted to ask: How was it to their glory that God permitted Paul to suffer for them? Simply this: If God allowed Paul to endure so much as the consequence of his work with the Gentiles, this was evidence of how important God figured this work to be. One of the prominent fruits of Paul's labors was the three years he spent with the Ephesians (cf. Acts 20:31).

Appreciation Of The Mystery—3:14 – 21

> (14) For this reason I bow my knees to the Father of our Lord Jesus Christ, (15) from whom the whole family in heaven and earth is named, (16) that He would grant you, according to the riches of His glory, to be strengthened with might through His Spirit in the inner man, (17) that Christ may dwell in your hearts through faith; that you, being rooted and grounded in love, (18) may be able to comprehend with all the saints what {is} the width and length and depth and height—(19) to know the love of Christ which passes knowledge; that you may be filled with all the fullness of God. (20) Now to Him who is able to do exceedingly abundantly above all that we ask or think, according to the power that works in us, (21) to Him {be} glory in the church by Christ Jesus throughout all ages, world without end. Amen.

14. **For this reason I bow my knees to the Father of our Lord Jesus Christ,.** For this reason (i.e., all the things he has mentioned in 2:11 – 3:13), Paul kneels in prayer to God the Father. There are many positions for prayer, but all of them ought to express humiliation and lowly supplication. I am convinced that too many Christians are simply too casual as they engage in worship today. Formalism is certainly wrong, but so is a thoughtless and careless attitude about our worship to God. When is the last time you

Chapter Three: Glory and Praise

actually bowed your knees to the Father? Paul, like the rest of us, are, in our connection with Christ, permitted to pray "to the Father."

15. From whom the whole family in heaven and earth is named,. The *family* or "household of God" (2:19), the "kingdom of God," i.e., the "whole building" (2:21), is under consideration here. This family consists of God, the "ministering spirits" or angels, the saints who are alive on planet earth, and those who have passed from this earthly existence and now reside in the Hadean realm. Everything else is the kingdom of darkness (cf. I Corinthians 6:9-11; Galatians 5:19-21; Colossians 1:13). Every day the praise of *the entire church in heaven and on earth* is offered to God the Father, the Son, and the Holy Spirit.

16. That He would grant you, according to the riches of His glory, to be strengthened with might through His Spirit in the inner man,. Paul was praying that out of the wealth of His glory, God would strengthen them with power *through* or *in connection with* the Holy Spirit, who dwells in them *individually* (I Corinthians 6:19,20) and *collectively* (I Corinthians 3:16), to be strong in the inner man as they comprehend the promises the Father has made to them in Christ. The "inner man," which is equal to the heart, soul, and mind (Matthew 22:37), is contrasted with the "outward man" or physical body (II Corinthians 4:16). It is this inner man that has been made alive in Christ Jesus (2:5), and all this in our connection with the Holy Spirit.

17. That Christ may dwell in your hearts through faith;. This is not another gift. It is a continuation of what is mentioned in verse 16. As we are strengthened with power in connection with the Holy Spirit, Christ dwells in our hearts through or *in connection with* faith. Faith, of course, comes from hearing the word of God (Romans 10:17), which, in turn, is the "sword of the Spirit" (6:17). It seems Paul is here speaking of that process that has to do with growing in "grace and knowledge of our Lord and Savior Jesus Christ" (II Peter 3:14-18). **That you, being rooted and grounded in love,**. The Ephesians, like all Christians, had been *rooted* and *grounded* in love. These two words are derived from two different conceptions—one borrowed from the process of nature and the other from architectural parlance. For a plant to be healthy, it must have good roots, and for a building to be sound, it must have a good foundation. These roots and this foundation are God's *love* for us in Christ. As our appreciation for God's love for us increases—as a plant whose roots grow wide, deep, and strong in the soil of that love, and as a foundation upon which a sound structure can be built—our love expands for God the Father, Son, and Holy Spirit, for brothers and sisters in Christ, for neighbors, and even for our enemies (cf. I John 4:7-21).

18. **May be able to comprehend with all the saints what is the width and length and depth and height—**. The immediate purpose of all that Paul has prayed for on their behalf is now stated. He wanted the Ephesians (and all Christians) to grasp or understand the width, length, depth, and height (i.e., *all aspects*) of Christ's love.

Chapter Three: Glory and Praise

19. **To know the love of Christ which passes knowledge;.** Just as our hearts and minds are guarded by a faith in God that produces a peace that surpasses all understanding (Philippians 4:7), there is a knowledge that comes from our experience of Christ's love for us that surpasses the knowledge we have of Him intellectually. **That you may be filled with all the fullness of God.** We have now reached the climax of Paul's prayer for the Ephesians and, by extension, all saints everywhere. He wants Christians to be filled with all the fullness (blessings, grace, etc.) that is ours "of," *with respect to*, God. This all derives from God because He is who He is. This is very similar to the idea conveyed in Colossians 2:9,10, which says: "For in Him dwells all the fullness of the Godhead bodily; and you are complete in Him, who is the head of all principality and power." In other words, our completeness is connected to Christ, in whom the fullness of the Godhead dwells bodily (cf. John 1:16).

20. **Now to Him who is able to do exceedingly abundantly above all that we ask or think, according to the power that works in us,.** In his prayer, Paul has asked much for the Ephesians. Nevertheless, he is firmly persuaded that God can do much more than we ask or ever think or conceive in our minds. This power has no limits in that it is "above all." In association with this omnipotence, God's grace, which is actually "the power that works in us," saves us from our past sins (2:8) and makes us spiritually "alive" (2:1) through the gospel of Jesus Christ (Romans 1:16.).

21. **To Him be glory in the church by Christ Jesus throughout all ages, world without end**. May worshipful praise and adoration be rendered to God,

the Father of our Lord (v. 14), because of the splendor of His wonderful and magnificent attributes (i.e., power [1:19; 2:20], wisdom [3:10], mercy [2:4], love [2:4], grace [2:5-8], etc.) made manifest in connection with the church, the glorious body of Christ, and in connection with Christ Jesus, its exalted head. This glory is to be God's now and forever. **Amen**. When the Holy Spirit inspired Paul to write these glorious words of praise to God, he was moved by that same Spirit to express his wholehearted approval by his use of the solemn "Amen."

CHAPTER FOUR
Spiritual Gifts

The first three chapters of this letter dealt with doctrine. Starting with this chapter, Paul embarks upon the practical application of the truth stated in the first three chapters. In other words, he now tells these Christians how they ought to live.

Walk In Unity—4:1-6

> (1) I, therefore, the prisoner of the Lord, beseech you to have a walk worthy of the calling with which you were called, (2) with all lowliness and gentleness, with longsuffering, bearing with one another in love, (3) endeavoring to keep the unity of the Spirit in the bond of peace. (4) {There is} one body and one Spirit, just as you were called in one hope of your calling; (5) one Lord, one faith, one baptism; (6) one God and Father of all, who {is} above all, and through all, and in you all.

1. **I, therefore, the prisoner of the Lord,**. What he says here is similar to what he said in 3:1, but the expression "for you Gentiles" is missing. He is not bringing to mind his suffering for their sakes, but his faithfulness to the Lord. **Beseech you to have a walk worthy of the calling with which you were called,**. Like all Christians, these brethren were called to faith by the gospel that Paul preached (II Thessalonians 2:14). Of course, faith without works or a "worthy walk" is nothing other than dead faith (James 2:26). True faith must show itself by true devotion to the

Lord, and Paul is simply exhorting these Christians to live faithfully (cf. Romans 12:1).

2. **With all lowliness and gentleness,**. These are characteristics of walking worthily. Lowliness (humility) and gentleness (meekness) are attitudes of the mind that are naturally connected. The opposite of lowliness would be pride and self-assertive arrogance. The opposite of gentleness is violence. **With longsuffering,**. Longsuffering (patience) is a part of walking worthily and is closely associated with lowliness and gentleness, but is here introduced by itself. It means not taking swift vengeance nor inflicting speedy punishment. It is prompted by our remembrance that we were called when sinners, and that the wonderful relationship we have in Christ is proof of God's longsuffering. **Bearing with one another in love**,. This is the outworking of all these other things. Forbearing the faults and failings of others is the obligation our Lord demands of us. This kind of love is mentioned in I Corinthians 13.

3. **Endeavoring to keep the unity of the Spirit**. Faith comes by hearing the word of God (Romans 10:17), which, in turn, is the sword or implement of the Spirit. Consequently, we, who are to speak the same thing (I Corinthians 1:10) and walk by the same rule (Philippians 3:16), are not surprised to be admonished to maintain the unity of the Spirit. This unity or "sameness" is articulated in the word the Holy Spirit has revealed to us in the Bible. Conversely, all human teachings, inventions, and institutions are occasions of discord, stumbling, and division in the religious world today. **In the bond of peace**. Any

Chapter Four: Spiritual Gifts

unity that does not secure peace between believers is not of the Spirit.

4. **There is one body,**. Paul is writing of the universal church of Christ (i.e., the "My church" of Matthew 16:18). This is made absolutely clear in Ephesians 1:22,23 and Colossians 1:18. The church (i.e., the Christians) at Ephesus were part of this one body. They had been added to it by none other than the Lord Himself (Acts 2:47). **And one Spirit,**. The body animated (I Corinthians 12:13) and guided (Romans 8:14) by the one Spirit cannot be divided. **Just as you were called in one hope of your calling;**. We are "called" by the gospel of Jesus Christ, who said: "I am the way, the truth, and the life. No one comes to the Father except through Me" (John 14:6). The only hope of salvation and eternal life the world has is through Jesus. (The reader is referred back to 1:18 for a further explanation of *hope*.)

5. **One Lord,**. This one Lord is Jesus Christ, crucified, buried, risen, exalted, and invested with all authority in heaven and earth. **One faith,**. Some argue that this is subjective faith. I disagree and think Paul is writing of objective faith, which is "the faith" of Jude 3. **One baptism;**. At the time Paul writes this letter, there is only one baptism, which would be baptism in water for the remission of sins, and there is absolutely nothing divisive about it. Consequently, there are not three different ways of administering it (sprinkling, pouring, and immersion). It is a burial or immersion (Colossians 2:12) in water (Acts 8:36) in the name of Jesus for the remission of sins (Acts 2:38). It puts one into Christ (Galatians 3:27).

6. **One God and Father of all, who is above all, and through all, and in you all**. Notice that this passage

is not saying *one God who is the Father.* Under consideration is the *one God and Father of all*, that is, our heavenly Father. "All" equals "the household of God" (2:19) and, therefore, constitutes all those who make up the *one body*. No matter what angle one looks at the "one body" or "all," who constitute us believers, it is God the Father who is *above, through,* and *in* us all.

Gifts—4:7–16

> (7) But to each one of us grace was given according to the measure of Christ's gift. (8) Therefore He says: "When He ascended on high, He led captivity captive, and gave gifts to men." (9) (Now this, "He ascended"—what does it mean but that He also first descended into the lower parts of the earth? (10) He who descended is also the One who ascended far above all the heavens, that He might fill all things.) (11) And He Himself gave some {to be} apostles, some prophets, some evangelists, and some pastors and teachers, (12) for the equipping of the saints for the work of ministry, for the edifying of the body of Christ, (13) till we all come to the unity of the faith and the knowledge of the Son of God, to a perfect man, to the measure of the stature of the fullness of Christ; (14) that we should no longer be children, tossed to and fro and carried about with every wind of doctrine, by the trickery of men, in the cunning craftiness by which they lie in wait to deceive, (15) but, speaking the truth in love, may grow up in all things into Him who is the head — Christ—(16) from whom the

Chapter Four: Spiritual Gifts

whole body, joined and knit together by what every joint supplies, according to the effective working by which every part does its share, causes growth of the body for the edifying of itself in love.

7. **But to each one of us grace was given according to the measure of Christ's gift**. The measure of Christ's gift from the Father (speaking of His humanity) was "the name above every name" (Philippians 2:9). In connection with all the power that was given to Him in heaven and earth (Matthew 28:19), He has given each one of us grace or gifts as He has seen fit. Some of these were miraculous gifts (cf. I Corinthians 12:11) and some were offices (v. 11). In this manner, Paul was given the grace or gift of being an apostle to the Gentiles (3:2,7).

8. **Therefore he says: "When He ascended on high, He led captivity captive, and gave gifts to men."** The giving of these gifts was dependent upon His ascension into heaven. The citation is from Psalm 68:19. "Captivity" itself (sin and death) was captured by the victorious Christ and He divides the spoils with His followers (cf. Colossians 2:15 and I Corinthians 15:57).

9. **(Now this,** These words introduce a statement that will explain the preceding verse. **"He ascended"**—. This implies a previous descent, which has to be from heaven, as Jesus said, "No one has ascended to heaven but He who came down from heaven, that is, the Son of Man who is in heaven" (John 3:13). **What does it mean but that He also first descended into the lower parts of the earth?** Ascent does not always imply descent, as it does here. For example,

the fact that Elijah ascended into heaven does not imply that he previously came down from heaven. But, Paul here speaks of Christ, who "made Himself of no reputation, taking the form of a servant and coming in the likeness of men" (Philippians 2:7).

10. **He who descended is also the One who ascended far above all the heavens, that He might fill all things.)** The One who "fills all in all" (1:23) is the One who is able to "fill all things." He who first *descended* so as to take upon Himself flesh and shed His blood for the remission of sins, has now *ascended* back into heaven where He rules supreme over the nations and is the head of His church. In connection with this He gives gifts to His inheritance.

11. **And He Himself gave some to be apostles, some prophets, some evangelists, and some pastors and teachers,.** Paul here numerates the various gifts and positions of leadership used by the Lord to promote unity in His body. His great plan for edification and unity began with the *apostles*. Jesus originally called twelve men as apostles (Matthew 10:2-4). The word apostle means "a messenger or one sent on a mission," and this is the purpose of the apostles of Christ. They were to take the gospel to the whole world (Matthew 28:19; Mark 16:15,16). These special men (with the exception of Judas who was later replaced by Matthias) had an essential part in establishing the unity to be found in Christ's church. Paul, of course, was included in this number because he was an apostle of Christ to the Gentiles (Acts 9:15,16; I Thessalonians 2:6). All of these apostles preached the same gospel and called upon all to unite in connection with the death, burial, and resurrection

of Jesus Christ (I Corinthians 15:1-4). The *prophets* were special spokesmen for God who received divine revelation from the Holy Spirit (I Corinthians 14:5, 29-33). This promoted unity for "no prophecy of Scripture is of any private interpretation, for prophecy never came by the will of man, but holy men of God spoke as they were moved by the Holy Spirit" (I Peter 1:20,21). The work of unity was further established by giving some to be *evangelists* (Acts 21:8; II Timothy 4:5). An evangelist was a preacher of the gospel. These men, like everyone else, were under obligation to "speak as the oracles of God" (I Peter 4:11). In doing so, they would promote the unity that word called for. Then Paul mentions *pastors* and *teachers*. Each local church of Christ was to have its own pastors and teachers. The pastors (or shepherds) are elsewhere identified as *elders* (Acts 14:23; 20:17; Titus 1:5; James 5:14) and *bishops* (I Timothy 3:1; Philippians 1:1; Titus 1:7). While overseeing the local church, these men fed the flock spiritual food (Acts 20:28). With their special qualifications (I Timothy 3:2-7; Titus 1:5-9), they were the kind of men who could keep unity and peace within the congregation. One of their qualifications was "able to teach" (I Timothy 3:2). They, along with others, had the ability to teach. Therefore, the apostles, prophets, evangelists, pastors, and teachers represented God's gifts to the church. Of course, it must be understood that this list was not intended to be exhaustive (cf. I Corinthians 12:28).

12. **For the equipping of the saints**. Every Christian needs to be equipped for service to Christ. The previous gifts are given for this purpose. **For the work of the ministry,**. When properly equipped, they are able to devote themselves to ministering to the

needs of others. In fact, every household of Christians ought to imitate the example of the house of Stephanas, who devoted themselves to the ministry of the saints (I Corinthians 16:15). A preacher is a minister of the gospel (Colossians 1:23; II Corinthians 3:6), but all Christians, not just preachers, are to devote themselves to ministering, which includes both the physical and spiritual needs of people. **For the edifying of the body of Christ**. When the gifts Christ gave to the church are doing their work, and getting Christians to do their work, then the body of Christ is going to be built up, as it grows in numbers, knowledge, piety, and good works.

13. **Till we all come to the unity of the faith and the knowledge of the Son of God**. According to 4:3, we already have a unity which needs only to be kept or guarded. Paul here begins to tell us about something that still needs to be attained. The ultimate goal or purpose of all these gifts is to lead us to the unity of the faith and the knowledge of the Son of God. Unity of the faith was the goal of the early church and should be the goal of the church today. There can never be unity with a denominational concept of "many faiths," because the unity that God accepts comes only through the knowledge of the Son of God, who is "the way, the truth, and the life" (John 14:6). **To a perfect man, to the measure of the stature of the fulness of Christ;**. The goal is further discussed and considers the end result. The aim of every faithful Christian is to be more like Christ. The word "perfect" means *full-grown*, and suggests maturity. The only way Christians can be sinlessly perfect is to be forgiven through Christ (I John 1:7). However, we can strive every day to measure up to the stature of the

fulness of Christ, and this is what pleases God. In this process, one can grow from an unskilled diet of milk to a mature diet of meat, able to discern both good and evil (Hebrews 5:12-14). The knowledge of Christ mentioned here is precise, personal knowledge of Christ, not merely a knowledge of who He is, but a close personal relationship and a profound understanding of Him, the kind that comes with understanding what Paul is writing about Him in this epistle.

14. **That we should no longer be children, tossed to and fro and carried about with every wind of doctrine, by the trickery of men, in the cunning craftiness by which they lie in wait to deceive,**. Without such special gifts, the saints would remain immature children who would be tossed about like something on the sea (perhaps a small boat or wave) driven by the wind. The wind here represents the various false doctrines of the false teachers, who were crafty and tricky. As one matures on the one true doctrine of Christ, he cannot be fooled by these teachers and their doctrines: "On Christ the solid rock I stand, all other ground is sinking sand."

15. **But, speaking the truth in love,**. Truth and love must be joined together. It is possible to speak the truth, but not out of love, and this is very hurtful. Truth without love will repel people. However, true love can never be devoid of the truth. It is not true love to allow someone to go to hell to avoid hurting their feelings. Those who speak the truth "in love" are interested in the ones who are being taught. **May grow up in all things into Him who is the head—Christ—**. No longer children but mature or grown up in Christ Jesus, who is the head of the body. The idea here is

not identity but intimacy. As we serve Him, pray unto Him, and learn of Him, we grow into Him. As Paul wrote in Philippians 1:21, "For me to live is Christ, and to die is gain."

16. From whom the whole body, joined and knit together by what every joint supplies, according to the effective working by which every part does its share, causes growth of the body for the edifying of itself in love. The "from whom" in this verse is Christ. His spiritual body (the church) is totally dependent upon His headship. Here Paul (as in I Corinthians 12) illustrates the church by the make-up and functioning of the human body. Christ, as the head of His body, wants every member of His body joined and knit together in unity. When this happens, His prayer for unity (John 17) is answered, and His spiritual body grows. Each member (or part) is called upon to do its share under the headship of Christ. Unfortunately, this truth is lost on the modern church which places too much emphasis on an office or offices and too little on the work required of every member of the body. The church builds itself up in love when everyone is working to make increase of the body. People who are busy usually have little time for quarreling.

The New Man—4:17–24

> (17) This I say, therefore, and testify in the Lord, that you should no longer walk as the rest of the Gentiles walk, in the futility of their mind, (18) having their understanding darkened, being alienated from the life of God, because of the ignorance that is in them, because of the hardening of their heart; (19)

Chapter Four: Spiritual Gifts

who, being past feeling, have given themselves over to licentiousness, to work all uncleanness with greediness. (20) But you have not so learned Christ, (21) if indeed you have heard Him and have been taught by Him, as the truth is in Jesus: (22) that you put off, concerning your former conduct, the old man which grows corrupt according to the deceitful lusts, (23) and be renewed in the spirit of your mind, (24) and that you put on the new man which was created according to God, in righteousness and true holiness.

17. **This I say, therefore, and testify in the Lord, that you should no longer walk as the rest of the Gentiles walk, in the futility of their mind,.** Paul here calls on the Gentile brethren to walk differently from the unconverted Gentiles, who do not let Christ direct them as head, but follow their own think-sos. This would take a lot of courage for the Ephesian Christians. They lived in the shadow of the glorious temple of Diana and with the multitude of her worshippers. To refuse to associate in the practices of their former friends took much conviction and courage. Today, it still takes a lot of conviction and courage to *no longer walk as the rest of the Gentiles walk*. Social drinking, lewd movies, night clubs, dancing, gambling, and many other things are very much a part of our modern society. As followers of the Christ, we must not walk in these things.

18. **Having their understanding darkened, being alienated from the life of God, because of the ignorance that is in them, because of the hardening of their heart;.** The world considers itself too wise to believe the things revealed in the Bible.

But, as Paul wrote elsewhere, "Professing themselves wise, they became fools" (Romans 1:22). They have allowed satan to blind their minds to the gospel (II Corinthians 4:4), and are, therefore, alienated from the life of God. This alienation occurs for two reasons: (1) the ignorance that is in them, and (2) the hardening (callousing) of their heart.

19. **Who, being past feeling,**. Sin is like anesthesia. At first, it is offensive and our conscience revolts against it. However, if we do not get away from it, it soon becomes less offensive and will finally overpower us. We could also compare it to freezing to death. The cold numbs its victims and they are doomed, but feel no pain. Being *past feeling* is the last stage before destruction. If one is never bothered by his conscience, he is in terrible peril. **Have given themselves over to licentiousness, to work all uncleanness with greediness**. Those who lose all feeling of guilt readily enter into licentiousness (cf. Romans 1:26-32). *Licentiousness* is a term that includes adultery, fornication, immodesty, shameless dress and speech, indecent behavior, etc. All these things are quite natural for one who has cast aside the feelings of conscience. Nothing is more terrible than the loss of shame. Immodesty should embarrass or anger us. If it does not, then we only need to remove the checks of circumstances to complete our descent into sin. These non-Christian Gentiles do not hesitate to involve themselves in uncleanness. They desire the pleasures of sin, and go greedily after them. This kind of greediness is usually associated with the love of money which Paul says is "a root of all kinds of evil" (I Timothy 6:10).

Chapter Four: Spiritual Gifts

20. **But you have not so learned Christ,.** Paul now reminds the Ephesian Christians, who were mostly Gentiles, that they are called to be different from the other Gentiles he just mentioned. What has made the difference? The opening of their hearts to learn of Christ.

21. **If indeed you have heard Him and have been taught by Him, as the truth is in Jesus:.** When one hears of Christ and allows His teaching to permeate the heart, the obeying and doing of truth is the result.

22. **That you put off, concerning your former conduct, the old man which grows corrupt according to the deceitful lusts,.** Paul taught that one went through a complete change when converted to the Lord. This requires that one "put off...the old man." Consequently, "if anyone is in Christ, he is a new creation; old things have passed away; behold, all things have become new" (II Corinthians 5:17). We should notice that the old man is corrupted by *deceitful lusts*. In other words, the things lusted for in this world promise thrills and satisfaction. Instead, they bring disappointment, shame, disgrace, and contention. Our old man—our former life before we obeyed the gospel—was becoming more and more corrupt (cf. II Timothy 3:13). Age and experience usually do not improve sinners. In fact, their consciences become duller and habits of evil become even more firmly fixed.

23. **And be renewed in the spirit of your mind,.** It is not enough to put off the old man, the old man must be replaced with something new. The only way one's life will change is to have a new mind: "For as he thinks in his heart, so is he" (Proverbs 23:7). Elsewhere Paul teaches that this transformation

comes about by the renewing of our minds (Romans 12:2). *Be renewed* is in the present imperative and is, therefore, a continuous duty and process. *The spirit of your mind* is the spirit that directs your mind. Before conversion it was disobedient. Now, it is a spirit of meekness, humility, and obedience.

24. **And that you put on the new man which was created according to God, in righteousness and true holiness**. The new man, or new nature, is a creation of God (II Corinthians 5:17; Ephesians 2:10). With God's help we can improve ourselves. We can "put on" the new man like one puts on a garment. We do not have to be the same old detestable person we once were. We can put on the "new man," who will live "soberly, righteously, and godly in the present age" (Titus 2:12). In other words, those who are Christ's have crucified the flesh with its passions and desires (Galatians 5:24).

Do Not Grieve The Spirit—4:25-32

(25) Therefore, putting away lying, each one speak truth with his neighbor, for we are members of one another. (26) "Be angry, and do not sin": do not let the sun go down on your wrath, (27) nor give place to the devil. (28) Let him who stole steal no longer, but rather let him labor, working with his hands what is good, that he may have something to give him who has need. (29) Let no corrupt communication proceed out of your mouth, but what is good for necessary edification, that it may impart grace to the hearers. (30) And do not grieve the Holy Spirit of God, by whom you were sealed for the day of redemption. (31) Let all bitterness, wrath, anger, clamor, and evil speaking be put

away from you, with all malice. (32) And be kind to one another, tenderhearted, forgiving one another, just as God in Christ also forgave you.

25. Therefore, putting away lying, each one speak truth with his neighbor, for we are members of one another. Created in righteousness and true holiness, certain obligations are placed on the Christian. This verse begins a series of seven practical exhortations concerning the walk of the Christian. The admonition to put away falsehood and speak the truth is always very hard to keep, but is repeatedly commanded in the New Testament (4:15; 5:9). Since the general theme of this chapter is unity, speaking truth to one's neighbor is important. Speaking lies can destroy peace and harmony faster than anything else. Paul reminds the Ephesians that they are members of one another, and to lie to each other would be like one member of the body fighting another member of the body. God's people—of all people—ought to be able to trust one another. Remember, lying is one of the things that God hates (Proverbs 6:16,17).

26. "Be angry, and do not sin": do not let the sun go down on your wrath,. This is a quote from Psalm 4:4. It is not a command to be angry, but a caution not to sin when angry. People often do things when they are angry that they would not normally do. While this is not a command to be angry, neither is it a prohibition of anger. Sometimes anger is necessary. Paul felt anger (Acts 13:9,10; 23:3) and so did Jesus (Mark 3:5). It would be impossible to live and never be stirred within one's emotions; however, the Christian must keep his emotions under control. While anger may be justified at times, it must be speedily cooled down. It should subside the same day it arises. When the sun goes down, our anger ought to be gone. If anger is held very long, it turns into malice, hatred, resentment, and the desire for revenge.

27. **Nor give place to the devil**. All this, in turn, gives a place (opportunity) to the devil to lead us into transgression. And while there is definitely a connection between anger and giving place to the devil, there are also other ways we can give a place to the devil. Some examples would be: (1) meditating upon lustful things, (2) thinking on what we think is our unfair share of earthly riches, (3) reading books, watching television, or going to movies that undermine faith and morals.

28. **Let him who stole steal no longer, but rather let him labor, working with his hands what is good, that he may have something to give him who has need**. It may seem strange that Christians would have to be told not to steal. But stealing is not uncommon. Some folks who never think of themselves as thieves are actually involved in stealing. They cheat on taxes, drive hard bargains, misrepresent products, loaf on their employer's time, short an employee's time, cheat on examinations, etc. Paul says let him who stole—regardless of how he did it, or what he stole—steal no more. Of course, the best antidote for stealing is honest labor. Work is not just for selfish gain, but to help others. We do this not by stealing from the rich to give to the poor. We do this by being gainfully employed and sharing our bounty with those who are in need. This passage is not an authorization for Communism. This verse

commands private generosity and assumes private ownership of property. If we don't own anything, we can't give it away. Communism, on the other hand, destroys private ownership and makes all things state property.

29. **Let no corrupt communication proceed out of your mouth, but what is good for necessary edification, that it may impart grace to the hearers**. Christians must carefully control their speech at all times. Paul is warning the Ephesians not to let any speech that is rotten and corrupt go out of their mouths (cf. 5:4; Matthew 12:36,37). Words carry with them the personality and thoughts of the speaker. They can do evil or good. The Christian must use his words for good things, such as giving instruction, encouragement, and correction.

30. **And do not grieve the Holy Spirit of God, by whom you were sealed for the day of redemption**. Israel grieved the Holy Spirit by their sins in the wilderness and in the land of Canaan (Isaiah 63:10). We grieve the Holy Spirit by wicked deeds and rotten speech. We grieve Him when we violate the commandments He has given us through the apostle Paul in this epistle. Holiness is always sensitive. Therefore, we should not be surprised to learn that the Holy Spirit by whom we were sealed is sensitive. For comments on being sealed with the Holy Spirit until the day of redemption, see 1:13,14.

31. **Let all bitterness, wrath, anger, clamor, and evil speaking be put away from you, with all malice**. *Bitterness* is an evil attitude which refuses to forgive or be forgiven. It manifests itself in sharpness, harshness, spitefulness, and resentment. This sin

closes all doors to reconciliation. The *wrath* and *anger* in this context represent an explosion of one's temper that is sinful, the kind that produces uncontrolled words and actions. *Clamor* is loud speaking, boasting, and quarrelling. With clamor there is no room for kindness. *Evil speaking* is from the Greek word *blasphemia*, and is often used to describe those who speak injuriously against God, as well as one's own fellowman. *Malice* is ill will, the desire to injure. Those who hold malice are wicked and depraved with a heart full of hatred. It is a sad state of affairs when disciples of Christ exhibit these "old man" traits. We must work hard to put away from us these sins by being "renewed in the spirit of [our] minds" (4:23), putting on the "new man." (4:24).

32. **And be kind to one another, tenderhearted, forgiving one another, just as God in Christ also forgave you**. The word *kind* is usually used to describe God. It describes one who is virtuous, good, mild, and pleasant. It manifests a tender attitude toward others to the point of being concerned and considerate toward their needs. Elsewhere Paul calls this "brotherly kindness" (II Peter 1:7). The word translated *forgiving* in this passage does not just mean to release from guilt. It also means to be gracious, kind, and benevolent. Someone might ask, "How can I be kind, tenderhearted, and forgiving toward one who has wronged me?" This is an "old man" question. The motive for Christian goodness and forgiveness is different from that of the world. Out in the world, people are good because "it pays." They get something in return. The Christian is good and forgiving toward our fellow men because God *in Christ* has forgiven us. We realize how much we are

Chapter Four: Spiritual Gifts

indebted unto God; therefore, we forgive the small offenses our neighbors commit against us. Although there can be no greater motivation for kindness, tenderheartedness, and forgiveness than this, we must also recognize that if we don't forgive, we are committing spiritual suicide (Matthew 6:15). This is the reason Christ taught his disciples, in the Lord's prayer, to "forgive our trespasses as we forgive those who trespass against us.

CHAPTER FIVE
How to Walk

Walk In Love—5:1-7

(1) Therefore be followers of God as dear children. (2) And walk in love, as Christ also has loved us and given Himself for us, an offering and a sacrifice to God for a sweet smelling aroma. (3) But fornication and all uncleanness or covetousness, let it not even be named among you, as is fitting for saints; (4) neither filthiness, nor foolish talking, nor coarse jesting, which are not fitting, but rather giving of thanks. (5) For this you know, that no fornicator, unclean person, nor covetous man, who is an idolater, has any inheritance in the kingdom of Christ and God. (6) Let no one deceive you with empty words, for because of these things the wrath of God comes upon the sons of disobedience. (7) Therefore do not be partakers with them.

1. **Therefore be followers of God as dear children.** After calling upon the Ephesians to be kind, tenderhearted, and forgiving like God, Paul begins this chapter by asking them to follow God as dear children. God has set the perfect example of forgiving through His Son: "that is, that God was in Christ reconciling the world to Himself, not imputing their trespasses to them" (II Corinthians 5:19), and all are called on to imitate His example. To do this we must follow as "dear children." Paul is not calling on these

Chapter Five: How to Walk

Christians to be childish, but rather, to be humble like children (cf. Matthew 19:14). To be converted and become like children is the only way to enter the kingdom of heaven (Matthew 18:3).

2. **And walk in love, as Christ also has loved us and given Himself for us, an offering and a sacrifice to God for a sweet smelling aroma**. It is not enough to say we love our brethren. Love must be set in motion. To walk in love requires continuous motion and action. And what kind of love does Paul require? The kind illustrated by Jesus, the perfect example when He went to the cross for all: "who died for us, that whether we wake or sleep, we should live together with Him" (I Thessalonians 5:10; II Timothy 2:11; I John 4:9). His offering had a "sweet smelling aroma" to God, which means that it pleased Him. When Christians walk in love with the spirit of sacrifice in their actions, they also are pleasing to God. This represents the way we are to follow in His footsteps: "For to this you were called, because Christ also suffered for us, leaving us an example, that you should follow His steps" (I Peter 2:21).

3. **But fornication and all uncleanness or covetousness, let it not even be named among you, as is fitting for saints;**. Motivated by Christ's love, the Christian is to flee fornication, lustful unclean living, and greedy desires. In fact, these things are not even to be mentioned in any positive way, as the world does. Among Christians, these things should be mentioned only to condemn them.

4. **Neither filthiness, nor foolish talking, nor coarse jesting, which are not fitting, but rather giving of thanks**. They must also avoid base and

lewd conduct, foolish talking, and jests with double meanings, which do not come up to the standard Christ has set for Christians. Jesting refers to speech that is nimble-witted, or easily turned, especially toward a bad meaning. So often the jesting of the world is based on double meanings. Jokes are created that can be taken with two meanings—one harmless, the other shady. Many comedians think they are not funny unless they utter a few such jokes. Such is never fitting for the Christian, and he will avoid all this kind of speech. A tongue turned loose in foolish talk and coarse jesting will "defile the whole body, set on fire the course of nature; and is set on fire by hell" (James 3:6). The same tongue that can do all this (James 3:1-12), when bridled (James 1:26), can also give thanks to God, and this is what Paul wishes for them to do.

5. **For this you know, that no fornicator, unclean person, nor covetous man, who is an idolater, has any inheritance in the kingdom of Christ and God.** Paul gives a second reason why all evil practices should be avoided. In addition to the fact that such is not fitting, he reminds the Ephesians that those who engage in such acts will not inherit the kingdom of Christ (i.e., eternal life or heaven). Why? These evils are of the devil, and those that live by them are cut off from God. These things represent the world, and make those who practice them an enemy of God: "Adulterers and adulteresses! Do you not know that friendship with the world is enmity with God? Whoever therefore wants to be a friend of the world makes himself an enemy of God" (James 4:4). We seem to think idolatry is something that only affects heathens. Conversely, the Bible teaches us that idols

Chapter Five: How to Walk

are not just to be found on pagan altars, but they exist in the hearts and minds of well-educated people as well (cf. Ezekiel 14). The apostle John warns Christians to keep themselves from idols (I John 5:21). In his Corinthian letter, Paul instructs them to flee from idolatry (I Corinthians 10:14). In this passage and in Colossians 3:5, he informs his readers that idolatry is something that can affect us all.

6. **Let no one deceive you with empty words, for because of these things the wrath of God comes upon the sons of disobedience**. Gnosticism, a religion already causing problems for Christians, taught that what the body does has no effect on the inner man. Thus, those who advocated this religion believed it was fine to engage in all these unclean sexual acts. However, Paul refers to such teaching as "empty words," and warns about being deceived. In Colossians 2:8, he wrote, "Beware lest anyone cheat you through philosophy and empty deceit, according to the tradition of men, according to the basic principles of the world, and not according to Christ," and in Romans 1:18, "For the wrath of God is revealed from heaven against all ungodliness and unrighteousness of men, who suppress the truth in unrighteousness." Deception is still one of the devil's most effective tools (Genesis 3:4; II Corinthians 11:3), and the Christian must always be on guard against it. The devil does not play fair!

7. **Therefore do not be partakers with them**.

Walk In Light—5:8-14

(8) For you were once darkness, but now {you are} light in the Lord. Walk as children of light (9) (for the fruit of the Spirit {is} in all goodness, righteousness, and truth), (10) proving what is acceptable to the Lord. (11) And have no fellowship with the unfruitful works of darkness, but rather expose {them}. (12) For it is shameful even to speak of those things which are done by them in secret. (13) But all things that are exposed are made manifest by the light, for whatever makes manifest is light. (14) Therefore He says: "Awake, you who sleep, arise from the dead, and Christ will give you light."

8. **For you were once darkness, but now you are light in the Lord. Walk as children of light.** To help these Christians see where they were, compared to where they are now, Paul uses a common illustration—light and darkness. God and His kingdom are always referred to as light. On the other hand, the devil and his kingdom are always referred to as darkness: "He has delivered us from the power of darkness and translated us into the kingdom of the Son of His love" (Colossians 1:13). The apostle Peter referred to how Christ "called [us] out of darkness into His marvelous light" (I Peter 2:9). When converted, the Christian becomes the light of the world (Matthew 5:14). In other words, the Christian is not just in the light, he is light, just as he was not just in darkness, but was darkness. Christians keep the darkness out by walking as children of light.

9. **(For the fruit of the Spirit {is} in all goodness, righteousness, and truth),**. When Christians are walking as children of light, they will be bearing the fruit of the Spirit. Instead of those wicked things

mentioned in verses 3 and 4, they will be demonstrating goodness, righteousness, and truth. The contrast is as different as day and night or light and darkness.

10. **Proving what is acceptable to the Lord**. (See Romans 12:2).

11. **And have no fellowship with the unfruitful works of darkness, but rather expose them**. The Christian, who is light, must have no association with the works of darkness. Such works are called "unfruitful" because they bear no fruit for goodness, righteousness, and truth. In addition to not having any association with the unfruitful works of darkness, the Christian is to go a step further and expose them. This will serve to warn others. Satan tries to make the works of darkness appear to be light, but this is a lie that must be exposed by the truth of God's word. Satan, himself, appears as an angel of light (II Corinthians 11:14).

12. **For it is shameful even to speak of those things which are done by them in secret**. Paul continues his warning. They must keep themselves pure for God. They do this by: (1) refraining from associating with darkness, (2) exposing the author of darkness—the devil, and (3) refusing to even speak of the shameful sins committed by them in secret: "men loved darkness rather than light, because their deeds were evil" (John 3:19). A Christian must not contaminate his mind with such filth. In so doing, we "abstain from every form of evil (I Thessalonians 5:22), and avoid being influenced by those who are evil (I Corinthians 15:33).

13. **But all things that are exposed are made manifest by the light, for whatever makes manifest is light**. One of the characteristics of light is to reveal or expose. Isn't there a vast difference between things at night and in the day? We stumble in the darkness and lose our way, but in the light all becomes visible. Many hated Jesus and His followers because they exposed their sins (John 3:19), and this is still true today. When one is accustomed to darkness, the light becomes very uncomfortable.

14. **Therefore He says: "Awake, you who sleep, arise from the dead, and Christ will give you light."** The Lord will not give enlightenment to those who are spiritually dead. Paul said the same thing to the Romans: "And do this, knowing the time, that now it is high time to awake out of sleep; for now our salvation is nearer than when we first believed" (Romans 13:11). The Christian must not slumber. He must be active, and the Lord will gladly give him light.

Walk In Wisdom—5:15-21

> (15) See then that you walk circumspectly, not as fools but as wise, (16) redeeming the time, because the days are evil. (17) Therefore do not be unwise, but understand what the will of the Lord {is}. (18) And do not be drunk with wine, in which is dissipation; but be filled with the Spirit, (19) speaking to one another in psalms and hymns and spiritual songs, singing and making melody in your heart to the Lord, (20) giving thanks always for all things to God the Father in the name of our Lord Jesus

Chapter Five: How to Walk

Christ, (21) submitting to one another in the fear of God.

15. See then that you walk circumspectly, not as fools but as wise,. Once again Paul refers to the figure of walking. One can choose to walk in darkness and find much disappointment, foolishness, and death, or he can choose to walk "circumspectly" (carefully) in the light. In so doing, one is walking wisely.

16. Redeeming the time, because the days are evil. In order to do this, one must take advantage of every opportunity to use time wisely! Why? The times are evil. This is true of all generations. Beware of any inclination to call the days good. We are still living in a perverse generation (Acts 2:40). We will never be able to make a paradise of this sin-sick world. One is to have great confidence in the power of the gospel, but must remember that only a few of all men living at any one time have ever accepted the gospel. Some of the opportunities that come our way will only come once. We must be willing to seize the moment. Although we cannot go back and relive our past, we can take advantage of the moment. Paul regretted his past of persecuting the church (Acts 8:3; I Corinthians 15:9; Galatians 1:3), but this did not stop him from pressing on (Philippians 3:14). This is the kind of wisdom that Paul wants all Christians to walk in as we redeem (lay up for ourselves) the time.

17. Therefore do not be unwise, but understand what the will of the Lord is. Paul expands upon the wisdom he desired for the Ephesians. Because the days are evil and are filled with great temptations, the Christian must always beware of foolish, ungodly, time-wasting conduct. Instead, he is to keep before his mind at all times the will of the Lord. And what is the will of the Lord? That the Christian should keep himself from all the works of darkness.

18. And do not be drunk with wine, in which is dissipation; but be filled with the Spirit,. Drunkenness is condemned in both the Old and New Testaments (Proverbs 12:1; 23:29-35; Isaiah 5:11,22; Romans 13:13; I Corinthians 6:9,10; Galatians 5:21). Drunkenness brings *dissipation*. "Dissipation" is a translation of the Greek word *asotia*, and, according to Vine, means "prodigality, a wastefulness, profligacy," i.e., *reckless* and *unrestrained* living. The prodigal son supposed, like many today, that wild living (which no doubt included drunkenness) was just great. He eventually learned that such had destroyed his happiness and self-respect (Luke 15:11-32). Instead of being filled with wine, Paul calls on Christians to be filled with the Spirit (i.e., the Holy Spirit, the third person of the Godhead). Paul is talking to individuals who had already received the Holy Spirit upon conversion. Therefore, what he is talking about here is being under the influence of the Holy Spirit's teaching. Being "filled with the Spirit" is equivalent to being under the influence of (i.e., being guided and led by) the Holy Spirit. He directs us through His word, which he describes later as the sword (or implement) of the Spirit (Ephesians 6:17). Being under the influence of the Holy Spirit, as opposed to being under the influence of wine, which brings dissipation, is that one is filled with love, joy, peace, longsuffering, kindness, goodness, faithfulness, gentleness, self-control, etc. (Galatians 5:22,23). Being thus filled, believers will give jubilant

Chapter Five: How to Walk

expression of all this, doing what is mentioned in the next verse.

19. **Speaking to one another in psalms and hymns and spiritual songs, singing and making melody in your heart to the Lord,.** The term *psalms* in all probability has reference to the Old Testament Psalter. *Hymns* refer mainly to New Testament songs of praise to God and to Christ (cf. verse 14). Finally, *spiritual songs* probably refer to sacred songs about things other than direct praise to God or to Christ. The drunkard may mumble, moan, and curse, but the Christian that is filled with the Spirit will want to sing from his heart to the Lord. Since Paul mentions "speaking to yourselves," he is referring to the occasions when Christians are assembled together, and not to an individual singing alone. Singing "psalms, hymns, and spiritual songs" is one of the ways Christians are to be taught in the assembly. Those who refuse to sing, refuse to teach! The melody is to be made in their hearts—no mechanical instruments are mentioned (they were added centuries later). In fact, nowhere in the New Testament are Christians told to play anything other than the strings of their hearts.

20. **Giving thanks always for all things to God the Father in the name of our Lord Jesus Christ,.** "Be anxious for nothing, but in everything by prayer and supplication, with thanksgiving, let your requests be made known to God" (Philippians 4:6; I Thessalonians 5:18). God wants us to be thankful! When Jesus took notice that only one of the ten lepers who had been healed returned to thank Him, He said: "Were there not ten cleansed?" "But where are the nine?" (Luke 17:11-19). Where would you be classified—with the

one, or with the *nine*? Jesus is the only mediator between God and man (I Timothy 2:5), consequently, all prayers and thanksgivings must be in His name (John 14:13,14).

21. **Submitting to one another in the fear of God.** In the duty to be "submitting to one another," the verb *hupotasso* means "to subject or subordinate," and is parallel to "giving thanks always." The general principle is that Christians must be subject to one another. This voluntary yielding to others is to be a general characteristic of the Christian community and is urged elsewhere in the New Testament. For example, in Philippians 2:3, Paul says, "Let nothing be done through selfish ambition or conceit, but in lowliness of mind let each esteem others better than himself." This voluntary submission is based on the example of Jesus: "who, being in the form of God, did not consider it robbery to be equal with God, but made Himself of no reputation, taking the form of a servant, and coming in the likeness of men. And being found in appearance as a man, He humbled Himself and became obedient to {the point of} death, even the death of the cross" (Philippians 2:5-8). Jesus had always insisted that His followers would have a servant mentality in imitation of Him: "Yet it shall not be so among you; but whoever desires to become great among you, let him be your servant. And whoever desires to be first among you, let him be your slave—just as the Son of Man did not come to be served, but to serve, and to give His life a ransom for many" (Matthew 20:26-28). Furthermore, the apostle Peter instructed young men to submit to older men, and for all Christians to submit to one another (I Peter 5:4,5). This is to be done because they fear

Chapter Five: How to Walk

God (Christ). Some of the manuscripts read "fear of God," others read "fear of Christ." The teaching in all these manuscripts is the same—Christians are to submit to one another out of fear or reverence (Greek = *phobo*) for Christ, who is Himself God.

Husbands And Wives And Christ And The Church—5:22-33

> (22) Wives, submit to your own husbands, as to the Lord. (23) For the husband is head of the wife, as also Christ is head of the church; and He is the Savior of the body. (24) Therefore, just as the church is subject to Christ, so {let} the wives {be} to their own husbands in everything. (25) Husbands, love your wives, just as Christ also loved the church and gave Himself for it, (26) that He might sanctify and cleanse it with the washing of water by the word, (27) that He might present it to Himself a glorious church, not having spot or wrinkle or any such thing, but that it should be holy and without blemish. (28) So husbands ought to love their own wives as their own bodies; he who loves his wife loves himself. (29) For no one ever hated his own flesh, but nourishes and cherishes it, just as the Lord {does} the church. (30) For we are members of His body, of His flesh and of His bones. (31) "For this reason a man shall leave his father and mother and be joined to his wife, and the two shall become one flesh." (32) This is a great mystery, but I speak concerning Christ and the church. (33) Nevertheless let each one of you in particular so love his own wife as himself, and let the wife {see} that she respects {her} husband.

Note: In verses 22 through 33 Paul addresses the specific roles of husbands and wives. By placing the mutual submission of all Christians to one another in verse 21, before stating the specific submission of wives to their husbands mentioned in verses 22 through 30, it seems that Paul wants to remind all Christians, men and women, of their duty to be submissive to one another before reminding wives of their particular responsibility to their husbands in marriage. This puts specific, one-directional subjection in the context of general, mutual submission and relates specific duties, roles, and responsibilities to the general Christian concept of mutual submission. Unfortunately, some make the mistake of thinking mutual submission alone is in view in these verses, and, therefore, wives are not being called to a unique or distinct submission to their husbands. However, since verse 21 is a transition verse to the entirety of the section on household responsibilities, consistency would demand that the sections on children and parents and on servants and masters also speak only of mutual submissiveness and not different roles. Since this is self-evidently not so for the verses on children and parents, on the one hand, and masters and servants, on the other, the implication is that distinguishable roles and specific submission are taught in this section on wives and husbands. Therefore, the mutual submission to which all are called and that defines the larger context and sets the tone for what follows does not, therefore, rule out the specific and different roles and relationships to which husbands and wives are called by these verses. In this section on wives and husbands, Paul presents his teaching along three lines: (1) the role

Chapter Five: How to Walk

each has (submission, headship), (2) the attitude with which each fulfills his or her role (love, respect), and (3) the analogy of marriage to the relationship of Christ and His church.

22. **Wives, submit to your own husbands,**. Paul commands wives to "submit to" or be "subject to" their own husbands. The operative verb *hupotasso* reappears in verse 24, where Paul says wives are to submit to "their own husbands in everything," "just as the church is subject to Christ." We know this is the essence of the apostle's teaching to wives, since in Colossians 3:18 it is the totality of his charge: "Wives, submit to your own husbands, as is fitting in the Lord." Furthermore, this particular exhortation to the wife to submit to her husband is the universal teaching of the New Testament. Every passage that deals with the relationship of the wife to her husband tells her to "submit to" him, using this same verb (*hupotasso*): Ephesians 5:22; Colossians 3:18; I Peter 3:1; Titus 2:4f. Distilled down, the teaching is this: Wives be submissive to your husbands. What is meant by submission? In its simplest form, the wife *allows* her husband to be head. In other words, there is no way a man can carry out his God-given headship without a submissive wife! In this regard there are three types of wives: (1) Those that deny plain Bible teaching. These do not want to submit. (2) Those who believe what the Bible teaches on this subject, but do not practice it. They do this while giving lip-service to the need to obey the Bible teaching. (3) Those that believe the word of God and spend their lives practicing it. This last group may fall short, but they continue to try. Only this third group is pleasing to God. **As to the Lord**. Certainly, no Christian ought to resent being in subjection to Christ, and if husbands were what they ought to be, their wives should not

resent being in subjection to them. Nevertheless, even when all reasonable causes for voluntary subjection are absent (i.e., gentleness, kindness, wisdom, etc.), the wife is still obligated to be submissive to her husband *as to the Lord*. Marriage is something neither the female nor male ought to enter into lightly.

23. **For the husband is head of the wife, as also Christ is head of the church; and He is the Savior of the body.** In this verse, Paul gives the basis for his charge to the wives. The husband, he says, is head (*kephale*) of the wife *as* Christ is head of the Church. Husbands are given a perfect model to follow in Christ as Head and Savior of His body (the church). Christ will never do anything to harm the church, but will save it. Husbands exercising godly headship will never do anything to harm their wives, but will love, protect, and save them. They will save them from physical harm, from attacks on their character, from unhappiness (when possible), and from spiritual death. Jesus loved the church enough to die for it (Acts 20:28; Ephesians 5:25), and godly husbands will strive for this same kind of love (I Corinthians 13).

24. **Therefore, just as the church is subject to Christ, so let the wives be to their own husbands in everything.** Since husbands have such an awesome responsibility to care for their wives, Paul again calls upon the wives to be subject to their own husbands. When a church refuses to submit to its head, it becomes an unfaithful church, and the same can be said of a wife who is not submissive to her husband. She is not just to submit in the things she likes, or areas where she agrees, but "in everything."

Chapter Five: How to Walk

This phrase is all-encompassing. In other words, submission includes all aspects of life. This removes the misunderstanding that some may have that submission simply refers to sexual intercourse or some other narrow realm. Since by God's decree marriage partners are "one flesh," God wants them to function together under one head, not as two autonomous individuals living together. Since Paul is so concerned about this unity, we ought to be also. Paul does not add to the expression "in everything" that all disobedience is excepted (cf. Acts 5:29, "We ought to obey God rather than men"; cf. also Acts 4:19,20). This goes without saying! Nor does he mean to make her a robot and stifle her thinking and acting. Rather, he wants her thinking and acting to be shared with her husband (as his is to be shared with her), and for her to be willing to submit to his leadership *in everything*. Just as the church should willingly submit to Christ in all things, and, if it does so, will not find that stifling, demeaning, or stultifying of growth and freedom, so also wives should willingly submit to their husbands in all things, and, if they do so, will not find that stifling, demeaning, or stultifying. Does any of this mean that the husband can rule his wife insensitively? Certainly not! The idea that anyone in authority should "lord it over" those he leads is ruled out by Paul elsewhere (II Corinthians 1:24), just as Peter insists that elders must not lord it over those who are obligated to obey them (I Peter 5:3). Paul takes this for granted. The husband has no authority to speak bitterly against his wife (Colossians 3:19), he certainly has no authority to beat or abuse her. (Paul handles the question of the husband's misuse of power momentarily in his words to husbands.) The important thing for the wife to know is that she is subject to her husband in everything, that is, that her submission involves all aspects of their relationship.

Note: Many Christian women are heard to complain about preachers and teachers always "jumping on" the woman's role first. Their complaint is that men need to "get right" on this subject also. In truth, both men and women need to understand what it means to be a godly husband and godly wife, but it is interesting to note that instructions to husbands and wives in the New Testament always focus first on wives and their responsibility to submit to their husbands (Ephesians 5:22-24; Colossians 3:18; I Peter 3:1ff.). If the wife will not submit, the husband cannot lead! Both Paul and Peter reaffirm the role relationship God established by creation before they deal with how men and women should conduct themselves in the relationship. The doctrine (the divinely instituted form) must come first, then the practical application (i.e., how one lives within the relationship). This is an important lesson.

Furthermore, Paul always addresses those under authority before those in authority—wives before husbands, children before parents, and servants before masters (Ephesians 5:22—6:9); Colossians 3:18—4:1). The rationale for the first two of these relationships would seem to be that the divinely instituted relationship is best preserved when the divine order inherent in it is made plain by urging compliance on those under authority first, before addressing those in authority. The apostle may then command those in authority to exercise their authority with loving concern that does not run roughshod over those under authority, thereby tempting them to

Chapter Five: How to Walk

challenge or resist the divinely established relationship (cf. especially 6:4). Having established the divinely given character of the institution and the God-given roles, Paul then spells out the attitudes with which those in that institution should fulfill their respective roles.

25. **Husbands, love your wives, just as Christ also loved the church and gave Himself for it,.** On this backdrop, Paul now addresses husbands. Love appears six times in 5:25-33, and it denotes the husband's duty to his wife. It is interesting to note that the husband's role—his headship—was stated in the section addressed to his wife (verse 23), and not in the section addressed to him. In other words, Paul does not tell the husband, "Be head over your wife!" Instead, he commands him twice to love his wife (verses 25,28). The command for the husband to love his wife is illustrated by the analogy of Christ's love for the church, and by the way one loves his own body (verse 28), which is by nourishing and cherishing it (verse 29). In this verse, Paul emphasizes the self-giving, self-sacrificing character of the husband's love for his wife: it is to be like the love Christ had and continues to have for the church. It is with this kind of love that the apostle of Christ commands the husband to exercise his headship over his wife in everything.

26. **That He might sanctify and cleanse it with the washing of water by the word,.** Christ loved the church so much that He died for it, that is, He purchased it with His own blood (Acts 20:28). In doing so, "He became the author of eternal salvation to all who obey Him" (Hebrews 5:9). When we obey the gospel, which includes believing, repenting, confessing, and being baptized, we are added to the

Lord's church (Acts 2:47). In other words, when the penitent believer is baptized, he is baptized *into* Christ (Galatians 3:27), and *into* His death (Romans 6:3), where His blood was shed (John 19:34). How does one know this? "By the word," of course: "Since you have purified your souls in obeying the truth through the Spirit...having been born again, not of corruptible seed but incorruptible, through the word of God which lives and abides forever" (I Peter 1:22,23). This is consistent with Mark 16:15,16, which describes the process of salvation as being (1) a preaching of the gospel (or the word), (2) faith, (3) baptism, and (4) salvation. The "washing of water" clearly refers to baptism (cf. Hebrews 10:22; Titus 3:5), and the necessary conclusion one must make from this is that *all* the church (the sanctified and cleansed) had been baptized. Since Christ did all this *for* the church, husbands should be willing to do whatever is good and right *for* their wives.

27. **That He might present it to Himself a glorious church, not having spot or wrinkle or any such thing, but that it should be holy and without blemish.** The uniqueness of Christ's redemptive work on behalf of the church cannot be precisely imitated by the husband, but Paul seems to be teaching that just as Christ works to present His church to Himself as a glorious bride in a glorious marriage, so should the husband work to make his wife glorious and their marriage magnificent. The husband's love, like Christ's, was to be beneficial to his wife, just as Christ's love for the church is beneficial to it. Of this love, Chrysostom wrote: "Wouldst thou that thy wife should obey thee as the church obeys Christ? Do thou then care for her, as Christ for the church, even if

Chapter Five: How to Walk

thou must lay down thy life for her?—shirk not, shouldst thou suffer even this. Thou hast not yet matched all that which Christ hath done. For thou doest this after thou hast already won her, but he sacrificed himself for her that turned away from him and hated him; and when she was thus disposed, he brought her to his feet not by threats, or insults, or terror, or any such thing, but by this great solicitude. So do thou conduct thyself toward that wife of thine... Her that is the partner of thy life, the mother of thy children, the spring of thy joy, thou must not bind by terror and threats, but by love and gentleness."

28. So husbands ought to love their own wives as their own bodies; he who loves his wife loves himself. Seeing that Christ loved the church so much that he gave Himself up for it, men ought to also love their own wives as they do their own bodies. The love that Paul calls for here is *agape*—love that considers what is best for the one loved. Only when this kind of love is present can a husband love his wife as his own body. Generally speaking, we want what is best for our own physical bodies. When sick, we seek medical attention. When hot or cold, we seek comfort. When hungry, we obtain food. It is so natural to love ourselves that Christ used this as the standard by which we are to love our neighbor (Matthew 19:19). Paul wants the husband to become one with his wife to the extent that when he loves her, he love himself. Just as all of us who are thinking rationally seek the best for ourselves, the husband who truly loves his wife and is exercising the headship that God has ordained will seek the best for his wife.

29. For no one ever hated his own flesh, but nourishes and cherishes it, just as the Lord does

the church. The church is spiritually nourished and cherished by the Lord to the point that nothing can destroy it, not even the gates of hades (Matthew 16:18). When this kind of love is present, all other problems can be solved by both husband and wife.

30. **For we are members of His body, of His flesh and of His bones.** Before Paul approaches the one flesh concept concerning a husband and wife, as taught in Genesis 2:24, he establishes the Christian's relationship to Christ's body, the church. The "we" refers to Christians and represents members of His body, flesh, and bones. This is a very close relationship to Christ and other members of the body. It serves as a figure of unity, cooperation, concern, and love. This figure is discussed in full detail in Romans 12 and I Corinthians 12. When Eve was presented to Adam after being made from his side, he said: "This is now bone of my bones and flesh of my flesh; she shall be called Woman, because she was taken out of Man" (Genesis 2:23). This same kind of unity and oneness is used to show the closeness of those in Christ's church.

31. **"For this reason a man shall leave his father and mother and be joined to his wife, and the two shall become one flesh."** After discussing the oneness of members of Christ's body, Paul returns to the oneness of the husband and wife. At this point, he quotes Genesis 2:24, the first recorded law of marriage. There are three important demands mentioned in this verse for marriage: (1) The man will leave his father and mother, (2) he will be joined to his wife, and (3) together they will become one flesh. To *leave* his father and mother means he is to begin his

own home. The man and woman who leaves father and mother still loves them and respects their faithful teaching, but they must leave to establish their own home. Happiness in marriage cannot be found when one runs back home every time there is a ripple on the sea of marital bliss. Mistakes will be made, but, as a general rule, these should be worked out by the couple as they grow deeper in their love for one another. To be *joined* to his wife means that they stay together. The Greek word means to "glue upon, glue to, or to join one's self closely to." When two pieces of wood are well glued together, the wood will break before the glue-joint does. Likewise, in the marriage bond, the husband or wife should die before the marriage bond breaks. Becoming *one flesh* is more than the sexual act. The *henosis*—the making of two *one*—is brought about by the total commitment of two personalities, each to the other, in the closest relationship of the flesh, i.e., sexual intercourse. Nevertheless, sexual intercourse alone does not make the *henosis*. In case of rape and seduction, there is no mutual commitment. In cases of harlotry, the sexual intercourse which was designed by God to be experienced in marriage, as a part of the "one flesh" experience, does not establish an actual *henosis*, but simply a "one body" relationship (cf. I Corinthians 6:16). What a great concept from God! This is one of the blessings of His creation that man and woman are made that they can become "one flesh." But, how many married couples really believe this? For example, suppose we were to gather an audience of people and bring before them a healthy man. Then, we ask the audience, "Is it okay to cut this man's arm off?" Or, "How do you feel about cutting this man's body in half?" If they were to actually think we were serious, there would be a mob effort to prevent such a thing from happening. However, in the case of a married couple that has become "one flesh," they can be divided in our society today without much concern at all. In God's sight, however, He sees a couple as ONE, just as surely as He sees the oneness of an individual body.

32. **This is a great mystery, but I speak concerning Christ and the church**. Unbeknown to the people of Moses' day (i.e., "it was a `mystery'"), marriage was *designed by God* from the very beginning to be a picture or parable of the relationship between Christ and the church. Back when God was planning what marriage would be like, He planned it for this great purpose—it would give a beautiful earthly picture of the relationship that would someday exist between Christ and His church. And now, in the New Testament Age, the apostle Paul reveals this mystery, and it is simply amazing! This means that when Paul wanted to tell the Ephesians about marriage, he did not hunt around for a helpful analogy and suddenly discover that "Christ and the church" might be a good teaching illustration. No, it was much more fundamental than that. By inspiration, Paul understood that when God designed marriage, He already had Christ and the church in mind. This is one of God's great purposes in marriage—to picture the relationship between Christ and His redeemed people forever! If this is so, then the order Paul is writing of here (submission and love) is not accidental or temporary or culturally determined. It is, instead, part of the *essence of marriage*, part of God's original plan for a perfect, sinless, harmonious marriage. Therefore, here we have a very powerful argument for the fact that Christlike, loving headship and church-

Chapter Five: How to Walk

like, willing submission are rooted in creation and in God's eternal purposes, not just in the passing trends of culture.

33. **Nevertheless let each one of you in particular so love his own wife as himself, and let the wife see that she respects her husband.** Notwithstanding the fact that the original marriage law was intended to show the relationship between Christ and His church, its application to human marriage remains unchanged. The husband MUST love his wife and the wife MUST be in subjection to her husband by respecting his God-given authority.

Note: The traditional family, as defined by secular society, has assumed the husband to be the superior ruler and the wife to be the inferior servant. This is far to the right of what God has ordained in His word. On the other hand, the feminist movement has swung the pendulum far to the left in denying the family structure and roles God has ordained. Let us, as Christians, strive to speak and act "as the oracles of God" (I Peter 4:11), and "not be conformed to this world, but be transformed by the renewing of [our] mind[s], that [we] may prove [to a lost and dying world] what is that good and acceptable and perfect will of God" (Romans 12:2).

CHAPTER SIX
The Whole Armor of God

Children And Parents—6:1-4

> (1) Children, obey your parents in the Lord, for this is right. (2) "Honor your father and mother," which is the first commandment with promise: (3) "that it may be well with you and you may live long on the earth." (4) And you, fathers, do not provoke your children to wrath, but bring them up in the training and admonition of the Lord.

1. **Children, obey your parents in the Lord, for this is right**. The home does not stop with the husband and wife relationship, but is expanded to include children. The first commandment given to Adam and Eve after God made them in His image was "Be fruitful and multiply; fill the earth and subdue it" (Genesis 1:28). In Genesis 4:1, the Bible says, "Adam knew his Eve his wife, and she conceived and bore Cain." Consequently, rules for the home must include both parents and children. As he did in the husband and wife relationship, Paul first addresses the one who is commanded to be in subjection. In this case, it is the child. This obedience is to be done "in the Lord," and when children respond in the Lord, all is well. Elsewhere, Paul wrote, "Children, obey your parents in all things, for this is well pleasing to the Lord" (Colossians 3:20), that is, obeying parents in all things as the Lord has indicated children should (i.e., "in the Lord") is pleasing to Him. It is most unlikely

Chapter Six: The Whole Armor of God

that Paul meant that children were to judge whether or not the things their parents commanded were in harmony with the Lord's will. Most children would not be capable of deciding such things. Simply stated: The duty of the child is to obey. Of course, just as in the case of the wife, the child could refuse to do anything commanded that was contrary to God's will. There is no higher authority than Christ, and all rightful authority ultimately derives from Him. No one has the moral authority to command someone to circumvent God's laws.

2. **"Honor your father and mother," which is the first commandment with promise:.** In this verse, Paul is appealing to the Fifth Commandment (Exodus 20:12), but it is actually the first commandment with a specific promise attached to it. And what is the specific promise? Look at the next verse.

3. **"That it may be well with you and you may live long on the earth."** This promise was twofold: (1) *That it may be well with you.* Generally speaking, any child that obeys his parents will be spared many troubles and mistakes. He will also be spared much chastisement as well. The law of Moses actually permitted the stoning of a rebellious child (Deuteronomy 21:18-21). This should impress us with the fact that God considers incorrigibility a terrible thing. (2) *That you may live long on the earth.* This originally referred to the privilege of dwelling in the land of Canaan (cf. Deuteronomy 5:33; 6:2; 11:8,9; 28:36). Of course, this promise has a fulfillment in the present times. The child who obeys his parents will probably have better health, safer habits, wiser ways, and certainly the blessing of God to lengthen and enrich his life. Just think of all the children who have

dissipated their lives because they have refused to obey their parents.

4. **And you, fathers, do not provoke your children to wrath, but bring them up in the training and admonition of the Lord.** Paul gave the headship to the husband, and he now gives the responsibility of discipline to the father. This, no doubt, includes the mother, but all under the headship of the father. Parents who are unreasonably strict with their children often drive them from home into early, unwise marriages, juvenile gangs, or into the ranks of the hardcore incorrigibles. No parent should tease or repress children until they are in a rage. Foolishness is indeed bound up in the heart of a child (Proverbs 22:15). Consequently, the rod of correction is needed (Proverbs 13:24; 29:15,17), and a child will not long resent just punishment. Even godly parents are not perfect and will occasionally make mistakes with their children. Children who are loved will not hold this against their parents. But, unjust and continuous abuse (corporeal or verbal) inevitably leads to exasperation and discouragement and will be avoided by godly parents. *Training* means that parents are under divine mandate to train, educate, and chasten their children. Children are not just ours to enjoy and caress, but to train for this life and the life to come. *Admonition* refers to exhortation, urging, and warning. We need to teach our children not only the truth, but to urge them to live by it. Parents will do well to notice the attitude of entreaty and exhortation found in Proverbs 5:1ff. and 6:1ff.

Chapter Six: The Whole Armor of God

Servants And Masters—6:5-9

> (5) Servants, be obedient to those who are your masters according to the flesh, with fear and trembling, in sincerity of heart, as to Christ; (6) not with eyeservice, as men pleasers, but as servants of Christ, doing the will of God from the heart, (7) with good will doing service, as to the Lord, and not to men, (8) knowing that whatever good anyone does, he will receive the same from the Lord, whether {he is} a slave or free. (9) And you, masters, do the same things to them, giving up threatening, knowing that your own Master also is in heaven, and there is no partiality with Him.

5. **Servants, be obedient to those who are your masters according to the flesh, with fear and trembling, in sincerity of heart, as to Christ;.** The *servants* referred to in these verses were bond-servants or slaves (cf. Colossians 3:22-25). Even though Paul may have disliked the concept of masters and slaves, such was a fact of life in the world in which he lived. Therefore, he felt obligated to give spiritual instruction to those in such positions. This is analogous to the way Moses is represented by Jesus as having given instruction about what a man must do when he divorces his wife (i.e., "because of the hardness of your hearts") without thereby indicating, as those who asked the question were implying, that Moses approved of or encouraged divorce (cf. Matthew 19:7,8). Furthermore, Paul elsewhere indicates that a slave could properly become free (I Corinthians 7:21), therefore, he does not treat slavery as a divinely ordained institution, as he does that of

husband and wife and parent and child. Since many households had parents, children, and slaves, he continues his teaching on having a relationship that will please God. The civil law of that time gave masters authority over their slaves, and slaves were legally bound to obey. When one became a Christian, there may have been the feeling that one was no longer under obligation to obey his master. Paul teaches that the gospel of Christ does not automatically cancel slavery, but it does completely change the estimation of the slaves in the master's eyes. To the Romans, slaves were generally looked upon only as *things*. To the Christian master, they became *people*, and even *brothers* in the Lord, if the slaves were Christians. Also, Christianity changed the slave's estimation of his master. The service his master required became an opportunity to serve Christ, and to demonstrate the power of Christ in his heart. Lest he should be displeasing to his master the Christian served with the usual "fear and trembling," but he served even more earnestly lest he should be displeasing to his Lord, who was expecting him to be an obedient slave. (Although slavery has now been outlawed, the obligations of slave and master cannot longer be specifically obeyed. Nevertheless, in all of our earthly relationships, Christ must be the standard of authority. Consequently, one ought to recognize that the general principles articulated in the days of slavery are applicable to the employer/employee relationship.)

6. **Not with eyeservice, as men pleasers, but as servants of Christ, doing the will of God from the heart,**. Paul does not stop with asking slaves to obey, but specifies for them to obey "as servants of Christ"

Chapter Six: The Whole Armor of God

and "fearing God" (Colossians 3:22). With Christ as the standard, they will obey even if the master is not kind and good (cf. I Peter 2:18,19). With Christ as their model, Christian slaves will obey when the master is watching, and when he is not watching. This service will not be affected in any way—it will be absolutely genuine!

7. **With good will doing service, as to the Lord, and not to men,.** See the comments that are made on the next verse.

8. **Knowing that whatever good anyone does, he will receive the same from the Lord, whether he is a slave or free.** Those who serve with eyeservice, as men-pleasers only, will work when the master is watching, but when they can get by with it they will engage in fraud, laziness, deceit, etc. This is not true of the Christian servant. They "Have regard for good things in the sight of all men" (Romans 12:17), and they follow the rule: "And whatever you do, do it heartily, as to the Lord and not to men, knowing that from the Lord you will receive the reward of the inheritance" (Colossians 3:23,24). The Bible says, "For we must all appear before the judgment seat of Christ, that each one may receive the things done in the body, according to what he has done, whether good or bad" (II Corinthians 5:10). This fact is true whether one is a slave or free!

9. **And you, masters, do the same things to them, giving up threatening, knowing that your own Master also is in heaven, and there is no partiality with Him.** Masters are under obligation to exercise the same benevolent, conscientious acts toward his slaves that Christ requires of the slave toward the

master. He must give up threatening his slaves, knowing that the Lord of both slave and master is in heaven on His throne, and in the judgment that Christ shall conduct upon His servants, He will respect no man's earthly rank or title, but will reward or punish everyone according to his deeds. Those who are obedient and faithful to the Lord will be saved, but those who rebel in sin will be lost (Matthew 25:32-34). (The phrase "giving up threatening" carries the idea of moderating threats, relaxing threats, or omitting threats. Threats often produce more terror and hurt more deeply than stripes and lashings.)

The Whole Armor Of God—6:10-20

> (10) Finally, my brethren, be strong in the Lord and in the power of His might. (11) Put on the whole armor of God, that you may be able to stand against the wiles of the devil. (12) For we do not wrestle against flesh and blood, but against principalities, against powers, against the rulers of the darkness of this age, against spiritual {hosts} of wickedness in the heavenly {places}. (13) Therefore take up the whole armor of God, that you may be able to withstand in the evil day, and having done all, to stand. (14) Stand therefore, having girded your waist with truth, having put on the breastplate of righteousness, (15) and having shod your feet with the preparation of the gospel of peace; (16) above all, taking the shield of faith with which you will be able to quench all the fiery darts of the wicked one. (17) And take the helmet of salvation, and the sword of the Spirit, which is the word of God; (18) praying always with all prayer and

Chapter Six: The Whole Armor of God

supplication in the Spirit, being watchful to this end with all perseverance and supplication for all the saints — (19) and for me, that utterance may be given to me, that I may open my mouth boldly to make known the mystery of the gospel, (20) for which I am an ambassador in chains; that in it I may speak boldly, as I ought to speak.

10. **Finally, my brethren, be strong in the Lord and in the power of His might**. The word "finally" lets the reader know that Paul is getting ready to close this letter, and now desires to leave them something very special. In being "strong in the Lord," Christians must not trust their own strength. Instead, they must rely upon "the power of His might." God's power is the only true resistance against the devil. This power is in the "panoply" or "whole armor" of God. Without it, they have no chance of winning against satan.

11. **Put on the whole armor of God, that you may be able to stand against the wiles of the devil**. In describing the Christian's spiritual panoply, the apostle Paul uses the Roman soldier as an analogy. Those of his day would immediately be able to understand the effect of such an analogy because they were accustomed to seeing the Roman soldiers in their midst. For us to get a better appreciation of what Paul is saying, it will be necessary to explore the actual panoply of the Roman foot soldier. We will do this starting in verse 14. In this verse, Paul makes it clear from the very beginning that protection is not afforded one who simply puts on one piece of the panoply—he must put it all on. If just one part is missing, this is the place where the enemy will strike. Paul also makes it clear that the foe we fight against

is not an unskilled enemy—he is deceitful and will use every trick in the book. The devil is a murderer, without truth, a liar, and the father of lies (John 8:44), full of deceit, an enemy of righteousness, and a perverter of the right way (Acts 13:10), who can transform himself into an angel of light (II Corinthians 11:14), and goes about like a roaring lion, seeking whom he may devour (I Peter 5:8). Again, without the whole armor of God, one will not be able to stand against him, which brings up a very important point: Christians are called upon, not to run or retreat from the devil, but rather to stand and fight.

12. **For we do not wrestle against flesh and blood, but against principalities, against powers, against the rulers of the darkness of this age, against spiritual hosts of wickedness in the heavenly places**. This passage makes it clear that behind the physical confrontations we experience with our fellow human beings, there are unseen spiritual hosts of evil at work. There is an ongoing confrontation between the kingdom of God and the kingdom of darkness. The powers which are opposed to us, and against us, and making war on us are the very highest order of evil angels, those with great power, those who rule over the idolatrous and sinful men in this world of darkness. They are a wicked spiritual host that inhabits the heavenlies, that is, the regions of the air, from which they continually assault us and seek to get us to commit sin. This battle is unseen but real. If we do not guard our hearts, satan has the ability to fill them with evil thoughts (Acts 5:3). If we do not "gird up the loins of our minds," then satan can blind our eyes and lead us astray (II Corinthians 4:4; 11:3). The Bible warns us that through some "snare," satan can

Chapter Six: The Whole Armor of God

take us captive to do "his will" (II Timothy 2:26). This snare is evidently the devil's allurement (temptation) to do evil. Of course, this does not teach us that satan can force us to do his bidding against our own free wills, only that if we are not careful he can fool us or snare us through the "deceitfulness of sin" and the "deceivableness of unrighteousness" (Hebrews 3:13; II Thessalonians 2:10). Finally, the Bible clearly informs us that Christians, even in the 20th century, must not be ignorant of satan's "devices" (II Corinthians 2:11). Although we are told to put on the armor, as if to fight on a battlefield, we are told that our struggle is also a "wrestling." No armor is worn by wrestlers. Consequently, there is a mixing of metaphors in these verses, but correctly so. We *are* engaged in a battle, and all that is involved in this metaphor is important to understanding our spiritual battle with the forces of evil. We are also involved in a close, personal struggle with the forces of evil that is best described as wrestling. The close, hand to hand combat of the ancient battlefield could very well be described as wrestling, and is, therefore, not out of place in this verse.

13. **Therefore take up the whole armor of God, that you may be able to withstand in the evil day, and having done all, to stand**. This is the second time Paul tells the Ephesians to "take up" or "put on" the whole armor of God. However, the first time they were not fully aware of its importance. After giving a powerful description of the enemy, he says, "take up the whole armor of God, that you may be able to withstand in the evil day." Soldiers do not do battle every day, but the day of battle is the day of testing. A soldier who, on the day of battle, had not "taken up" his full armor, would be unprepared to stand against

and prevail over the enemy. Consequently, the "evil day" under discussion in this verse is the day of severe trial or testing, the critical moments in our lives when the devil and his sinister horde assault us fiercely. Seeing as one never knows when these crises will occur, one needs to be ready always. When the Christian makes all the preparations God has specified, then he will be able to "stand" and prevail against him, for the Bible tells us that if we resist satan, he will flee from us (James 4:7).

14. **Stand therefore, having girded your waist with truth,.** *Truth* here is not objective but subjective and is not, therefore, the Word of God, but truthfulness. The Christian is to be sincere and non-hypocritical. He puts away lying (Ephesians 4:25) and learns to speak the truth in love (Ephesians 4:15) as he demonstrates the fruit of the Spirit in his life (Ephesians 5:9). Paul is allegorizing the thick belt the Roman soldier placed around his waist. To this belt the soldier attached his dagger and sword. Furthermore, the breastplate was held in place by being attached to this belt. In addition, leather straps reaching to the knees hung from this belt and protected the soldier from sword strokes to that part of his body. What Paul was saying was that honesty and truthfulness are foundational in our fight against satan and his evil horde. The apostle Peter taught this same principle when he wrote that the very first thing a person needed to add to his faith was virtue or moral integrity (II Peter 1:5). According to Peter, moral integrity must precede a further knowledge of God's Word because without it one will never apply the truth of God's Word to his life. One cannot defeat satan and his horde without first being honest. **Having put on the breastplate of**

Chapter Six: The Whole Armor of God

righteousness,. *Righteousness* in an ethical sense is here meant (Ephesians 4:24; 5:9). In order to defeat the enemy, the Christian must lead a devout and holy life as he presents the members of his body as "instruments of righteousness to God" (Romans 6:13; 14:17). The breastplate was a very important part of the Roman soldier's battle gear. It protected his vital organs, particularly his heart, from serious injury. If we think in terms of the heart as representing the mind, as the Bible sometimes does, then we understand how the breastplate of righteousness protects the Christian soldier from the arrows of satan. Furthermore, awards the Roman soldier won were attached to the breastplate in medallion form for all to see. Likewise, when one looks at the Christian today, he ought to see the many medallions that reflect the righteous acts of the faithful Christian soldier. Clearly, then, unless the Christian puts on "the armor of righteousness on the right hand and on the left" (II Corinthians 6:7), and walks worthy of the Christian army into which he has been called (Ephesians 4:1), he can have no real defense against satan.

15. **And having shod your feet with the preparation of the gospel of peace;**. This is perhaps a difficult metaphor to understand. Just what Paul had in mind cannot be understood without some knowledge of the Roman soldier's footwear. The Roman soldier wore a thick-soled sandal with hobnails embedded on the underside for traction. The sandal was laced to the foot and lower leg with leather straps. During the winter months these straps were tied around leather leggings for warmth. Shod like this, the Roman soldier was able to quickly traverse various kinds of terrain. The Roman legions were notorious for their ability to quick-march fifty

miles in one day. Surprising their enemy by being where it was thought they could not be, the legions were prepared for battle on any kind of terrain, whether it happened to be the rough and rocky highlands or the hot and dry deserts. When the command came to stand and hold, the legionnaire was able to do so partly because of the traction he could get with his hobnailed sandals. In other words, the Roman sandal was both an offensive and defensive weapon. Likewise, the Christian soldier, having his feet shod with the preparation of the gospel of peace, is always ready to give an answer to every man that asks a reason for the hope that is in him (I Peter 3:15). Just as the Roman soldiers were ready for any set of circumstances that came their way, Christian soldiers, likewise, are "anxious for nothing" and know that "the peace of God, which surpasses all understanding, will guard [their] hearts and minds through Christ Jesus" (Philippians 4:6-7).

16. Above all, taking the shield of faith with which you will be able to quench all the fiery darts of the wicked one. Paul is alluding to the large shield used by the Roman foot soldier of his day. This shield was not the small round one used by the cavalry; it was, instead, four feet long, two feet wide and resembled a door. It was constructed of wood and wicker over which animal skins were stretched and the edges were studded with iron to protect the leather. The shield, in addition to providing the normal protection one would expect from a shield, was designed specifically to stop and extinguish the flaming projectiles of the enemy. The leather was stretched over the wicker so as to provide a space between it and the wood underneath. When the fiery arrows and

Chapter Six: The Whole Armor of God

darts passed through the leather and stuck to the wood underneath, they were extinguished. It was this very effect to which Paul was referring. In the devil's quiver there are all types of fiery missiles. The apostle mentions tribulation, anguish, persecution, famine, etc. All of these can start the fires of doubt, lust, greed, vanity, envy, etc. But when the Christian soldier takes up his shield (his belief or conviction or trust) he is able to quench all the fiery darts of satan and his army. The Christian knows that God is able to deliver him from every temptation (II Peter 2:9) and will always be faithful in that He will not allow him to be tempted beyond what he is able to endure and with every temptation will also make a way of escape (I Corinthians 10:13).

As we contemplate the strength and power God has designed into this shield, we are reminded of a battle technique used so effectively by the Roman soldiers. Upon approaching the enemy's ramparts, the Romans would be pelted with every kind of missile the enemy had at his disposal. In such circumstances, the soldiers were commanded to form the "movement of the tortoise." This was accomplished by closing ranks and locking shields in front, on the sides and over the top. The shields had hooks at the top, bottom and sides that allowed them to be locked together. When in the formation of the turtle the soldiers were practically invulnerable. Consequently, when spiritual soldiers of the cross lock their shields of faith together in spiritual combat, they are, as the apostle Paul wrote, "more than conquerors through Him who loved [them]" (Romans 8:37). He went on to say, "For I am persuaded that neither death nor life, nor angels nor principalities nor powers, nor things present nor things to come, nor height nor depth, nor any other created thing, shall be able to separate us from the love of God which is in Christ Jesus our Lord" (Romans 8:38-39).

The Christian soldier who steps out on the battlefield without his shield is committing spiritual suicide. This very foolish and hurtful process is described in I Timothy 6:9-10, which reads: "But those who desire to be rich fall into temptation and a snare, and into many foolish and harmful lusts which drown men in destruction and perdition. For the love of money is a root of all kinds of evil, for which some have strayed from the faith in their greediness, and pierced themselves through with many sorrows." Yes, it is unfortunate that there are Christian soldiers who are pierced through with satan's fiery darts. Wounded and dying they cry out that the Lord has not been faithful to them. On the contrary, it is they who have not been faithful to Him. It is they who have failed to take up the shield of faith. The fault is with them, not God.

17. **And take the helmet of salvation,.** The Roman soldier's helmet in Paul's time was very different than the skullcap type that is usually depicted by modern artists. The Roman soldier of the First Century and thereafter wore a helmet that flared out on the sides and back to protect the neck area as well as the head. If the soldier got careless or became weary and let his guard down, this helmet protected him from a sword stroke that would have otherwise been fatal. Likewise, the Christian who, either through carelessness or weariness, lets his guard down is still protected from the death blows of the enemy. As Christian soldiers we sometimes make serious mistakes (in other words, in a weakened state of faith, we sin), but isn't it

wonderful to know that "If we confess our sins, He is faithful and just to forgive us our sins and to cleanse us from all unrighteousness" (I John 1:9)? Although our shield of faith is the greatest defensive weapon we have in our entire panoply, in that it is able to quench all the fiery darts of the enemy, it is heartening to know that even when we fail to use it as God has designed it, we are still protected. The blow of the enemy still hurts and we may even be knocked to our knees, but the enemy's death stroke does not kill. Praise God through our Lord and Savior Jesus Christ!

In many instances the Roman soldiers placed some kind of plumage on the tops of their helmets, and when observed from a distance by the enemy they looked to be seven feet tall. Consequently, many adversaries were known to have fled just at the approach of the Roman legions. Frankly, with the panoply of God firmly in place, it would not surprise us one bit if our enemy was sometimes tempted to flee at our approach. In I Thessalonians 5:8, Paul refers to this helmet as the "hope of salvation." Realizing that the helmet of salvation protects us from our own weaknesses and carelessness, we confidently enter the affray knowing that we are going to be victorious with God's help (cf. Romans 8:14-17). **And the sword of the Spirit, which is the word of God**. The Spanish gladius, a two-edged sword which was used by the Romans during Paul's lifetime, was two feet long and two and one half inches wide, and was designed primarily as a thrusting weapon. With it, the Roman legions were successful in conquering the world. A great deal of skill was needed to master the gladius sword. It has been reported that the Roman authorities thought it needful for their soldiers to train for up to five years before they ever saw combat. Often the sword the soldier practiced with was twice as heavy as the one he would actually use in combat. Developing the strength to wield the heavier practice sword enabled the soldier to use the gladius sword very effectively. He also had to be broken from the natural human tendency to slash with the sword. As we have already mentioned, the gladius sword was designed for thrusting and it was this use of the sword that made it so deadly effective. Most of the armies the Romans fought against used curved swords designed primarily for slashing. Consequently, when the enemy soldier lifted his arm to slash with his sword, he left himself vulnerable under his arm where there was no protection from his breastplate. As the enemy soldier swung with all his might, the Roman soldier would block his swing with his shield as he stepped to the left where he would thrust forward with his short sword and ram it into the armpit of his opponent. Without practice the Roman soldier was destined to fail; but with it he conquered every enemy.

Likewise, "the word of God," which is actually "sharper than any two-edged sword" (Hebrews 4:12), requires practice if it is going to be used effectively. Therefore, in his instructions to Timothy, Paul wrote: "Be diligent to present yourself approved to God, a worker who does not need to be ashamed, rightly dividing the word of truth" (II Timothy 2:15). The skillful use of God's Word "belongs to those who are of full age, that is, those who by reason of use have their senses exercised to discern both good and evil" (Hebrews 5:14). When used skillfully, the sword of the Spirit pierces the heart (cf. Acts 2:37; 7:54). In order to defeat the enemy, the Christian soldier must learn to use the sword of the Spirit expertly.

18. **Praying always with all prayer and supplication in the Spirit, being watchful to this end with all perseverance and supplication for all saints—**. Although some think Paul is still using the military metaphor of the soldier's appeal to his General, we are of the opinion that Paul is now referring to something not available to the carnal soldier. The Christian soldier, unlike the Roman soldier, has at his disposal a means whereby he can continuously communicate (through Christ, of course) with the General (viz. God, the Father). Understanding the seriousness of his warfare, the Christian soldier is always (not just on special occasions) involved in prayer and supplication in harmony with the truths taught in God's Word (i.e., "in the Spirit"). As he fights the good fight of faith, the Christian soldier petitions for the fulfillment of definite needs with the understanding that the One to whom he appeals is not just interested and concerned, but loving too.

Praying for the fulfillment of one's own needs, as well as the needs of "all saints," requires that one must be acquainted with the specific situations that are taking place in the world today. Part of our problem today is that many Christians are uninformed as to what is happening and consequently they are not praying frequently and knowledgeably. Unalert or indifferent to what is happening in the world, their country, their town, their church, and their home, they have a very restricted prayer life. We must remember that if there is any fault it is not with God. We must repent and pray to God for forgiveness and that He keep us from temptation.

19. **And for me, that utterance may be given to me, that I may open my mouth boldly to make known the mystery of the gospel,**. Paul's request is not selfish! So many prayers are: "Lord, give me!" It is, of course, not wrong to ask for personal things, but our prayers must certainly not stop there. Paul felt the weight of responsibility of preaching the gospel (I Corinthians 9:16). However, it was not just enough to preach the gospel, he wanted to speak it "boldly." Why? Because that which had been a mystery needed to be revealed. The world needed to know that Jesus died, was buried, and arose from the dead so that both Jews and Gentiles might be saved and be ONE in Christ Jesus (Galatians 3:28). The gospel to the Gentiles was not a popular subject, and it took courage to go against the opposition of the Jews. Thus, Paul felt the need of prayers so that he could open his mouth and speak boldly. Today, society is more interested in entertainment, sports, and materialism than the gospel, but this must not keep Christians from spreading the "power of God unto salvation" (Romans 1:16), for the gospel represents lost humanity's only hope in eternity.

20. **For which I am an ambassador in chains; that in it I may speak boldly, as I ought to speak**. Paul, as we have already learned, is writing this letter from prison. He is in prison not for murder, theft, or insurrection, but because he dared preach the gospel of Christ. He asks that the Ephesians pray for him that he might "speak boldly, as I ought to speak."

A Gracious Greeting—6:21-24

Chapter Six: The Whole Armor of God

(21) But that you also may know my affairs {and} how I am doing, Tychicus, a beloved brother and faithful minister in the Lord, will make all things known to you; (22) whom I have sent to you for this very purpose, that you may know our affairs, and {that} he may comfort your hearts. (23) Peace to the brethren, and love with faith, from God the Father and the Lord Jesus Christ. (24) Grace {be} with all those who love our Lord Jesus Christ in sincerity. Amen.

21. **But that you also may know my affairs and how I am doing, Tychicus, a beloved brother and faithful minister in the Lord, will make all things known to you;**. This verse reminds us once again of Paul's great concern for others. He believed that these brethren would be deeply concerned about him being in prison, therefore, he sent word by Tychicus. What a great recommendation Paul gave this man! He is described as a beloved brother who was faithful in the Lord. Every faithful preacher of the gospel should desire this kind of description. Tychicus is mentioned in other places and was of great value to Paul and his work as a "faithful minister," "fellow servant," and messenger (Acts 20:4; Colossians 4:7; II Timothy 4:12; Titus 3:12).

22. **Whom I have sent to you for this very purpose, that you may know our affairs, and that he may comfort your hearts**. Surely, he was able to bring great comfort to the Ephesians, since he was faithful to Paul and the Lord.

23. **Peace to the brethren, and love with faith, from God the Father and the Lord Jesus Christ. (24) Grace be with all those who love our Lord Jesus Christ in sincerity. Amen.** Paul closes this wonderful letter with four of his favorite words: peace, love, faith, and grace.

Note: Paul did not fail in his mission, and neither must we. Like Paul, ultimately, victory is ours. With the full armor of God, we know that we are "thoroughly equipped for every good work" (II Timothy 3:17) and that we are "more than conquerors through Him who loved us" (Romans 8:37). As such, we are confident that "neither death nor life, nor angels nor principalities nor powers, nor things present nor things to come, nor height nor depth, nor any other created thing, shall be able to separate us from the love of God which is in Christ Jesus our Lord" (Romans 8:38--39). In other words, we know we have no excuse for failing to win the battles of life. By faith, we know we can do everything the Lord has determined that we should do (cf. Philippians 4:13). By faith, we know that "those who are with us are more than those who are with [our enemy]" (II Kings 6:16).

FAST FACTS ON THE BOOK OF EPHESIANS

APOLLOS AND PRISCILLA AND AQUILA (ACTS 18:24-28)

In Ephesus Priscilla and Aquila met questioned a Jew named Apollos concerning baptism. He had been baptized under John the Baptist's baptism. The problem with John's baptism was that it was related to the Mosaic sacrificial system, was only for Jews, and was not tied in any way to the sacrificial death of Jesus. John's baptism passed away with the Mosaic sacrificial system when Jesus died on the cross. Apollos knew about Jesus and believed in Jesus as the Messiah, and taught accurately about faith in Jesus, but his understanding of baptism was misplaced! His baptism united him with John and not with with Jesus. Priscilla and Aquila taught him *"the way of God more accurately"* (Acts 18:26). In the context of what Luke was describing, this must have related to baptism into Jesus. After Priscilla and Aquila straightened Apollos out regarding "the way of God," Apollos went on his way and powerfully debated and "confuted" (proved to be false or invalid) the Jews in open discussion.

TWELVE DISCIPLES BAPTIZED (ACTS 19:1-7)

After his brief discussion of Apollos, Luke informs us that Paul made his way to Ephesus (Acts 19:2) where he found about twelve disciples. As the discussion of Apollos had centered on his baptism, Paul's discussion with the disciples in Ephesus did likewise. On this occasion the discussion began with questions regarding the Ephesians having received the Holy Spirit. Their response was that they had never even heard of the Holy Spirit since their baptism was into John the Baptist's baptism. After hearing about the baptism of Jesus (Acts 2:38) they were baptized into Jesus and received the Holy Spirit. We are reminded that Peter had told the Jews on the Day of Pentecost that if they were baptized in the name of Jesus for the remission of their sins they would receive the Holy Spirit as a gift.

Why does Luke brings these two discussions on baptism together here in Acts 18 and 19? It must have been because he wanted to correct some false views regarding the baptism of John, and explain that Christians are baptized into Jesus, not John.

PAUL TEACHES IN THE SYNAGOGUE AND HALL OF TYRANNUS (ACTS 19:8-20)

For 3 months Paul debated and pleaded with the Jews in the Synagogue, but they were stubborn and refused to believe in Paul's message.

Paul then left and continued his teaching in the Hall of Tyrannus. Luke tells us that Paul preached in the Hall of Tyrannus for 2 years, and that all of Asia heard the Word of the Lord during that period. By this he meant that people from all over Asia (modern Turkey) heard the Word. Tradition has it that the Hall of Tyrannus was located in the North East corner of the Agora (market place) just across the street from the Great Theater. It is about this time period that Paul writes the Epistle 1 Corinthians to the church in Corinth.

Figure 2 is a map showing Asia, Ephesus, and the seven cities of Asia mentioned in Revelation.

PAUL AND EXTRAORDINARY MIRACLES IN EPHESUS (ACTS 19:11-21)

God confirms Paul's message with a number of extraordinary miracles. This led Paul into a clash with the seven sons of Sceva, a Jewish high priest in the area of the exorcism (casting out) of an evil spirit. The spirit acknowledged Paul and Jesus, but did no recognize the seven sons of Sceva and attacked those present. News of this spread throughout Ephesus and the name of Jesus was praised. Many of the citizens burned their magic books as a result of this experience and the message of the Word grew mightily. Many believed in Jesus because of this experience.

DEMETRIUS AND THE SILVERSMITHS IN EPHESUS (ACTS 19:23-41)

Demetrius, a silversmith in Ephesus stirred up a riot against Paul for damaging his silver idol business. Demetrius made idols of the Greek goddess Artemis in honor of whom Ephesus had centuries earlier erected an enormous and magnificent Temple in the City.

On the map of Ephesus (Figure 1) you will find the Temple to the North East of the map. On the map the

Temple is called the Temple of Diana which was the Roman name for the Greek goddess Artemis.

The crowd seized Paul, Gaius and Aristarchus, Paul's Macedonian traveling companions, and dragged them into the Great Theater. Some city officials, who were friends of Paul, begged him not to go among the crowd and speak up. When Alexander, a Jew, spoke up, the crowd got angrier (this indicated the tension between Jews and Greeks in Ephesus). The whole community was in an uproar. The town clerk quieted the crowd so they would not run into opposition with the Roman authorities. He suggested that Paul had niether harmed Ephesus, the temple keeper of the goddess Artemis, nor been sacrilegious toward Artemis. He instructed Demetrius to bring the matter before the regular city assembly. Acts 20:1-2 informs us that at that point Paul left Ephesus for Macedonia.

Ephesus in the years to come became a major Christian center, possibly the center of Christianity in the early second century. In the fifth century a large church was erected in Ephesus and named after the Apostle John. More New Testament letters are written to and about the church in Ephesus than to any other church in the first century.

PAUL AND THE EPHESIAN ELDERS (ACTS 20:17- 39)

While at Miletus Paul called the elders of the church in Ephesus to meet him in a touching experience. Paul reminded them of his ministry in Ephesus and of the message of grace through faith he had preached for both Jew and Greek. He informed them that he did not know what lay ahead for him other than that the Holy Spirit had warned him of imprisonments in every city where he preached. He told them that they "would not see his face again" which troubled them deeply. He warned them of false prophets and teachers and encouraged them to stay close to "God and the word of his grace". After prayer and tears, Paul left them.

The problem of false teachers in Ephesus must have been very real, for in almost every letter or writing addressed to or relating to Ephesus in the New Testament (Acts 20, Ephesians, 1 & 2 Timothy, 1, 2, 3 John, Revelation) there are warnings concerning false teachers and false doctrine.

FIGURE 1 – MAP OF EPHESUS

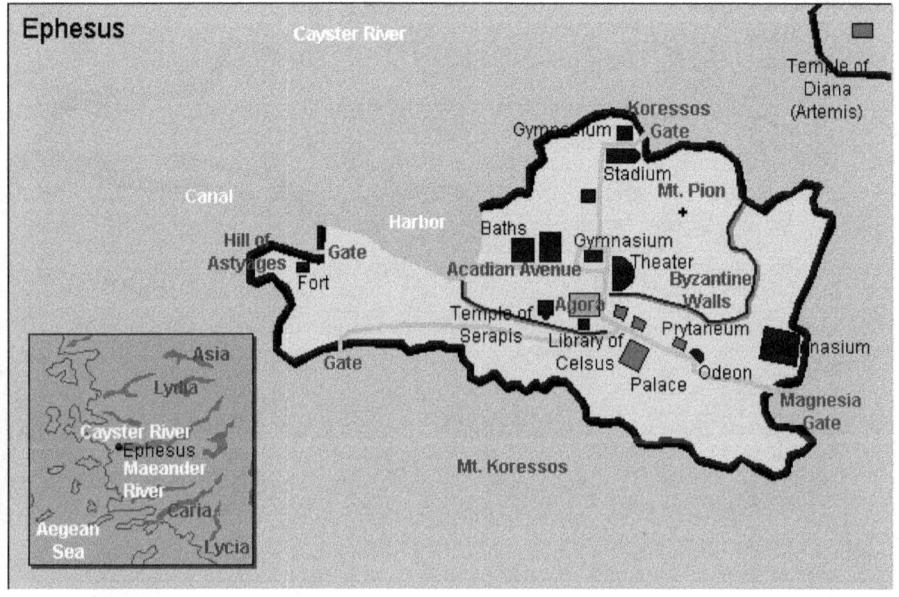

Figures

FIGURE 2 – SEVEN CHURCHES OF ASIA

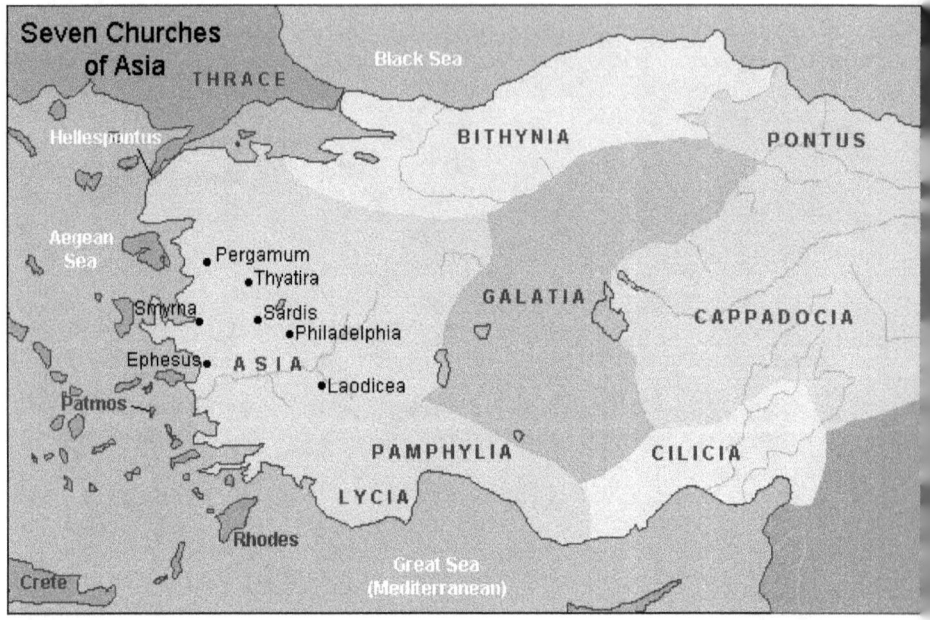

www.ingramcontent.com/pod-product-compliance
Lightning Source LLC
Chambersburg PA
CBHW071707040426
42446CB00011B/1958